They Cried Out To The Lord

31 Days of Prayer

for Parents of

Trans Identified Children

Mark Anderson Smith

Copyright

First published in Great Britain by Goal 31 Ltd, 2025
This print edition published in 2025 by Goal 31 Ltd
ISBN: 978-1-915183-02-6

Copyright © Mark Anderson Smith, 2025
All rights reserved.
No reproduction without permission.

The right of Mark Anderson Smith to be identified
as author of this work has been asserted by him
in accordance with sections 77 and 78
of the Copyright, Designs and Patents Act, 1988.

www.goal31.co.uk
books@goal31.co.uk

Scriptures taken from the Holy Bible, New International Version®, NIV®. Copyright © 1973, 1978, 1984, 2011 by Biblica, Inc.™ Used by permission of Zondervan. All rights reserved worldwide. www.zondervan.com The "NIV" and "New International Version" are trademarks registered in the United States Patent and Trademark Office by Biblica, Inc.™

Cover template from
bookcovermall.com

For Alan and Grace, and all who stood by us, encouraged us, and strengthened us

Other books by this author:

31 Days of Prayer series
31 Days of Prayer: Repent, for the kingdom of heaven is near
The Commands of Jesus
Preparing For Prison

Non-Fiction
Double Your Salary …without losing your soul!

Fiction
The Great Scottish Land Grab
Fallen Warriors

Contents

Introduction		7
Day 1	You Are Not Alone	15
Day 2	Let your hair grow back in	19
Day 3	I will not lie, unless...	23
Day 4	Be strong in the Lord	27
Day 5	A time to mourn	31
Day 6	Speaking the truth	35
Day 7	Shall I pursue them?	39
Day 8	A marathon not a sprint	45
Day 9	When your hopes are dashed	49
Day 10	Am I a coward at heart?	53
Day 11	Robbed of our children	59
Day 12	Heroes in their own story	63
Day 13	The belt of truth	69
Day 14	The breastplate of righteousness	75
Day 15	The gospel of peace	83
Day 16	The shield of faith	87
Day 17	The helmet of salvation	93
Day 18	The sword of the Spirit	99
Day 19	Pray in the Spirit	103
Day 20	Enough trouble	109
Day 21	Outside of time	115
Day 22	Speaking up	123
Day 23	Wolves in sheep's clothing	129
Day 24	Twenty years	135
Day 25	Plan to prosper	139
Day 26	If her father had spit in her face	143
Day 27	In your anger do not sin	149
Day 28	The strangest dream	155
Day 29	A sacrifice of praise	163
Day 30	Letting go	167
Day 31	They cried out to the Lord	171
Your Invitation		178
A Final Word		180
Resources		181

Introduction

*But when they cried out to the Lord,
he raised up for them a deliverer,
... who saved them.*
Judges 3:9

We are lost and confused, adrift in a leaking boat while a storm rages around us. So many parents have shared their stories of finding out their child identifies as trans and far too many mirror my own experience – of a sense of terror and helplessness as our child seeks to pursue something that defies understanding. Our child says they are not who they are. Years of parenting have given us a keen insight into who our child is and, in an instant, all that we thought true is upended. Some parents give in and as one father told me: "believe the lie until it becomes true." Others retreat, unable to cope with a traumatic event that threatens to destroy all their hopes and dreams for their child. For myself, I considered ending my life, something that other parents of trans identified children have also confessed to. Why? Our children are the literal future. If they and we have no future, then what is the point in struggling on? Yet at my darkest point I realised that to take my life would be an act of evil and I determined that I would not let evil have one more victory.

I'm estranged from my child. From all my children, as far as I can tell. There is only one child out of our three now adult children who now communicates with me at all, and that only briefly, by text, every three months or so. The others either refuse to let me know they are still alive or have forgotten their father even exists. None of them will tell me why. I've been told that my trans identifying child has cut me out of her life because I don't accept she is my son. And I don't accept that. I'll never accept that. Not because I hate her. Not because I don't love her, instead it is because it would be a lie, and how can I lie to my child? It breaks my heart that any of my children would want to go through their lives excluding me. I didn't have especially big dreams for our future relationships. Occasional phone calls where they'd tell me what they were up to. Being able to share with them what was going on in our lives – my wife, their mother and I. Meeting up at birthdays and maybe the occasional Christmas or New Year. Perhaps they'd even ask me for advice sometimes. Or I might ask them! That was all I dreamed of. And of course, as many of us parents hope for, one day, grandchildren. The future generations, slowly progressing down through time, carrying on our name and our line.

For my trans identifying daughter, it appears that the desire to have children of her own has not been considered. Instead, sterilisation may be on the cards. And that is bad enough, yet she wants more. She describes what she wants as healthcare. Yet cutting off her breasts to shape her body into a more masculine form does not sound like healthcare to me. Taking cross-sex hormones is not healthy and as far as I've been able to tell, is extremely dangerous. I need to be careful here though. This is not a book seeking to explain why so-called gender affirming treatments are dangerous. There already have been several excellent books warning us of the dangers of so called "gender affirming treatments" and I list some of them in the Resources section at the end. I highly recommend using these resources yourself. Perhaps here it is enough to say that I've read enough and researched enough to be convinced that we have been lied to. By our trans identifying children and by those who have affirmed them in their gender identities. We have been lied to by other Christians and churches, who have attempted to convince us to accept and affirm trans identities. We have been lied to by governments around the world, by doctors and therapists and the media and so, so many people. I am accused of saying that trans people do not exist. This is of course a clever deception itself. I believe that my daughter believes she is trans. I believe she exists. I do not accept that her perception of herself is valid or helpful. Not to her or anyone else.

We are being asked to ignore our instincts, to distrust our perceptions and put our trust in a set of beliefs. But can we trust those beliefs? How can we when trans and gender identity is self-contradicting. We are told gender identities are fixed. And that they are fluid. Both cannot be true. Historically, most young people desisted from a trans identity during puberty. It is only as our society has begun affirming our children that so many have persisted in believing they are trans. I believe we have to ground ourselves in reality, and the grittiest reality I've found is Jesus Christ. He described himself as the way and the truth and the life. I believe we need the guidance that Jesus offers to stay the course in this trans storm we parents face. We need this level of truth which was willing to be beaten and scourged and ultimately crucified for our salvation. We need life, the life which keeps us from our darkest instincts, protects us from thoughts of ending our lives, sustains us and nourishes us and enables us to not only continue living, but look forward and plan for the future.

Also, this is not a book giving advice on how to "fix" our children. Each child who identifies as trans may have complex reasons and experiences that have contributed to them choosing or latching onto the idea they might be trans. Our children need our love and help, though they may be unwilling to accept either our love or help. Some of you may be estranged, as I am, from your child. As those who are estranged, we are unable to even gently question or challenge or lead them to better understand themselves. This is a book for you – for parents of children who are lost and deceived and at risk of great harm.

I wrote this book as an attempt to help myself understand what I was going through as a parent with a trans identified child. I wrote it in the hope that by sharing my thoughts, sharing how God's word brings order to the confusion I've felt, that this might help you. As I've re-read and edited the chapters, I've often struggled to recall how one day I could write something that seemed so clear and full of hope when I'd once again plunged into a time of depression and grief. And then I've re-read another chapter that describes that sense of loss and confusion I am again feeling, and I've hesitated whether to share that with you. I don't want to drag you down into the depths with me, yet if I'm not honest about how I'm feeling, what I'm thinking, well, it seems to me that we've all been lied to far, far too much. Perhaps a little honesty would be good for us all.

I do not use what is now called preferred pronouns in large part because I see them as a lie. For my whole life pronouns indicated biological sex and I found them quite useful. Now, when I see pronouns given at the end of an email, I find myself asking whether the person is telling the truth or not.

I've been told my daughter has changed her name from the female name we gave her to a male name. One of the last messages she sent to me included an accusation that I "dead-named" her. I hope my child did not understand how cruel that was. For any parent to be presented with the possibility their child is dead is one of our worst nightmares. To have a living child attempt to convince us they are dead is an assault on our reality. I now understand this to be gaslighting, a manipulation technique that seeks to confuse and disrupt, to make us doubt our senses and intuition. There is a myth put out by some trans activists that our children are at a great risk of suicide if we do not affirm their identities. Any loving parent will struggle to resist this. Without any contradictory information, we can be led down a path where we are coerced into aiding and abetting in harming our child. The truth though is that it is those children and young people who have been affirmed and have received "gender affirming treatment" that are at a higher risk of taking their lives. Those children who are allowed to go through natural puberty, who are lovingly challenged, and encouraged to accept reality, they are likely to grow to accept their body as it is.

As far as I am aware, my child believes she is trans and appears unable so far to reconcile with those aspects of her body that contradict her belief. I hear she is planning to have her breasts removed. We don't really know why, perhaps the distress of gender dysphoria is driving her to do this. Despite my child indicating my daughter is no more and has been replaced by a son, my daughter is not dead. But we read in the accounts of Jesus that even a dead daughter can be brought back to life. Dead daughters and dead sons, they were brought to Jesus, or Jesus was brought to them and through amazing miracles, the child lives again. Yet I also know that Jesus will not heal or save every child. Either because the child refuses to accept help, or others intervene to lead the child astray or for reasons we may never understand in this life. This knowledge has almost crippled me at times. The awareness of possible outcomes and future suffering. I believe that we as parents have been betrayed. We have been lied to and sometimes lied about. It is as if we are living through a horror story and few if any will listen to us. We are grieving and yet cannot publicly express that grief. We grieve for the loss of our daughter. For the loss of the future we anticipated. We grieve that we are unable to do the things normal parents do such as help her get ready for college, provide support and be a part of her life even as she becomes ever more independent. And we grieve that our older children have cut us off and given us no opportunity to make things right with them. I have heard so many similar stories from other parents. Their experiences mirror my own.

I have felt trapped, as so many parents of children who identify as trans do. Unable to tell the story for fear. Fear of pushing our child away. Fear of putting a permanent wedge between us and them. Fear of losing other family members due to them choosing to affirm our daughter's trans identity and refusing to listen to our concerns. I've been afraid I might lose my job if I speak out about my concerns. I've had fear of being ostracised and shamed in public because I question why our child needs to take hormones or have surgery.

There is so much fear. And I have felt like a coward. Such a coward. For what have I done? What have I done to stop this, prevent it, change it? I can't remember now if I'd already been reading about cults, or was led to read about them after receiving the worst news I've ever been given. Was it cowardice that restrained me from immediately travelling up to fetch my daughter home, or was it wisdom that recognised that when you pull someone out of a cult, even and especially the cult of trans, that there is a real risk the moment they get a chance they will run right back? I don't know. Perhaps on this Earth, I will never know.

I began to wonder about writing another book in my 31 Days of Prayer series – a book for parents like us. Parents who are confused and lost and struggling and terrified. Maybe I could write that book and publish it and that might help someone else.

This is my attempt to do that. To encourage parents and maybe even other family members who so desperately need encouragement at this time. I have been making notes for months, noting down passages from the Bible when they felt relevant, and jotting down ideas as they came to me. After releasing my last book – *Preparing For Prison* – on my blog: goal31.substack.com, I set out to focus on this book, the title of which was not yet clear to me. Possibly, Transformed. Then Parents Transformed, or Transformed Parents. I played around with Transformation and Transfiguration and briefly even with Transgression. Then one morning in my daily reading of the Holy Bible I came across this statement: They cried out to the Lord. I knew I had found a title that encompassed what so many of us parents feel, even those who have never believed in God or known Jesus.

There is a saying that will be familiar to many of you: "There are no atheists in a foxhole." When bullets are flying, bombs are going off, and your child, whom you love so dearly is in danger, who among us will not cry out to our creator for help? And since for many of our children it can take long years for them to outgrow the trans identity, will our faith survive the drawn-out battle? Will we dig in for the long haul? Will we examine where we are weak and shore up our defences? Will we exercise and look after ourselves knowing that it is vitally important to love ourselves so that we can continue to love our child?

This book is not the answer to your prayers though I hope it points to the one who is, to Jesus. I've given the book the tagline: The Hope of God. Hope seems to be something we desperately need. Not a false hope. Instead an expectant hope. A patient hope. A hope that behind the scenes, in a realm we have little understanding of, our Father in heaven is working for our child's good, playing the long game. I have long found comfort in Paul's letter to the Roman church: "And we know that in all things God works for the good of those who love him, who have been called according to his purpose." All things. Even the nightmare of what our children plan to do to themselves. We cry out to the Lord for a swift delivery of our child from this trap they have placed themselves in. We cry out to the Lord for their protection. We cry out to the Lord for strength to carry on, for mercy, for forgiveness, for us and for our child. And over time our cry may mature, may gain new perspectives. Paul also writes in the same letter: "…suffering produces perseverance; perseverance, character; and character, hope." God could at any time make any of us do whatever he wants. He chooses not to, for the good of us all. And while we may want that power over our children, it would be the end of their free will and the end of their joy and kindness and delight. It may be that the suffering our children are going through, the suffering we experience as parents will transform us in the end as we persevere, as our character develops and as we discover a hope in God that stabilises our lives and brings us peace that calms the storm around us. If you have a child or relative who is struggling with a trans identity, may you know the hope of God and find peace in Him.

Yours in Christ

Mark Anderson Smith

Day 1

You Are Not Alone

"Be strong and courageous. Do not be afraid or terrified because of them, for the Lord your God goes with you; he will never leave you nor forsake you."
Deuteronomy 31:6

I've been a science fiction fan since a young age. I probably watched *Doctor Who* from behind the sofa. Although I stopped watching the series several years ago, I did follow the rebooted story from Christopher Eccleston through Matt Smith. Spoilers to follow!

At one point in the third series the Doctor and his companion travel to the end of time and meet Professor Yana. A recurring theme throughout the whole of the first few series of *Doctor Who* was that the Doctor was alone. We find out later that he destroyed his people – the Time Lords of Gallifrey – to save the universe and lived with the guilt of what he had done. He was the last of his kind, all alone in the universe. Until he met Professor Yana.

My wife and I felt all alone after our child came out as trans. Our other children withdrew from us until it was as if we were estranged from all three of them. We felt such shame and guilt, not knowing what we had done wrong. No-one would or could tell us. We didn't initially feel we could tell anyone else. Gradually we did, to the few family who were not also affirming our child's trans identity, to the pastor of our church and a few close friends. Eventually someone directed us towards an online support group and we were greeted with what are now familiar words: "Welcome to the group no-one wants to be part of.

We're glad you found us. None of us want to be here. We want you to know you are not alone."

If your child identifies as trans, you are not alone. There are thousands of parents in similar situations in the UK and perhaps tens of thousands around the world. Most of us are struggling. Most of us find ourselves unable to accept what is obviously not true. We desperately do not want our child to harm themselves. Although in recent months – as I write this in early 2024 – there has been a slight change in public perceptions, still there are a large number of people who are highly influential in the media insisting that the response to trans identity should be to accept and celebrate it. Politicians, journalists, even medical professionals. How can all these people not see what we see – our child, the child we always knew? How can they claim the impostor is the real person?

If you've seen those David Tennant episodes, you'll know that there is an opportunity for reconciliation, for two orphans to find each other and be a family again. Then the twist. The knife in the back. Professor Yana is revealed as the Doctor's sworn enemy: the Master. The Doctor is not the last of the Time Lords, Yana is an acronym for You Are Not Alone. I'll share later of an experience we had, someone who claimed to be there to help and I now think was a threat to our family. It is such a betrayal to think someone is on your side and then to find out they never were.

Throughout this nightmare we have been living, for over two and a half years now, there has been someone who has been faithful, who has been by our side the whole way, comforting us, giving us courage to continue, our Father in heaven.

When Moses spoke the words above to Israel, he was preparing them for battle, for war. If you read the surrounding passage in Deuteronomy 31, we see God himself promises to go ahead of the army, to destroy their enemies before them. I do not know where you are at in your situation. I am assuming you have a child who identifies as trans. You may not want to think of this situation as a war. To consider that preparing for battle is what you must now do. I cannot say that I have had this attitude from the start. Instead I confess I have despaired. I have lived in denial, hidden away. Been a coward. Not the whole way through, but I will not lie to you and pretend I am someone I am not. I have struggled and I am struggling. This is part of the reason I am writing this book – to help me do what has to be done, to learn how to pray for my child and this situation.

The Lord himself goes before you and will be with you; he will never leave you nor forsake you. Do not be afraid; do not be discouraged."
Deuteronomy 31:8

There is a repetition here in this encouragement given to the Israelite people. God confirms to them that he is with them, that he will not leave or forsake them. You may have felt abandoned, know that God has not abandoned you. Even though you may be terrified, we are told: do not be afraid; do not be discouraged even though this may be a long fight we are engaged in. Why would God say this unless it was true. And indeed, it was true. As Israel obeyed God, miracles happened. The walls of Jericho fell, not from siege engines or battering rams, but a miraculous earthquake. It is said that the sun stood still for a day while a battle raged, that while Moses held out his hands to God, the people of Israel prevailed against their enemy.

Who is your enemy? Not your child whom you love.

No, your enemy is something harder to define, more difficult to discern. It is an idea, implanted in your child's thinking. It has been pointed out to me that throughout this book I switch between using trans as an idea, or to describe, or as an entity itself. I feel that all of these are useful as trans is confusing, hiding its true nature from us, saying in one minute it is one thing and then insisting it is something else. Whether an idea or an entity or something else, I believe trans needs to be defeated, yet the battle is not ours, it belongs to God. And God has promised he will not leave our side in this battle. I hope you will join me as I try to understand what God is saying to us as parents, caught up in a fight we were likely not prepared for. I hope you will be encouraged, your faith will be strengthened. Ultimately, I hope we will see our children saved.

Father in heaven, thank you for the promises you gave to Israel before their battle. I do believe that you give the same promise to everyone who believes in Jesus – that you will not leave us or forsake us, that you go with us and are asking us to look to you for direction. May we ask of you, may we seek your guidance, may we knock hard on Heaven's door, and may you hear our prayers and answer us. You told Israel to be strong and courageous, make us strong, Father, give us courage to fight through prayer for our child. Let us take our fears and terrors to you and find comfort in you. Reassurance that you love our child more than we ever could. Protect our child, deliver them from harm. Amen

Day 2 — Let your hair grow back in

Then the Philistines seized [Samson], gouged out his eyes and took him down to Gaza. Binding him with bronze shackles, they set him to grinding grain in the prison. But the hair on his head began to grow again after it had been shaved.
Judges 16:21-22

For most of the first year after we found out our child identified as trans, I was bereft. I was never the mighty man that Samson was, yet I was successful in my own way. I had achieved a few things, accomplished some personal goals. I was providing for my family and while I knew I had flaws and faults, I was trying to be a better person. Then, in a period of days, it was as if everything of value was taken away from me. I still had my wife, my home, my job, yet even though each of my children lived on, it was as if they had all been kidnapped. Even worse, they had kidnapped themselves, and refused to name terms of release, to communicate with us. And the fear... The terror of what my youngest child planned to do to herself, and I was powerless to stop my child self-harming.

I've been told I jump to step ten when most people are still getting to grips with step one. Self-harm? You may not associate trans or gender identity with self-harm, why did I? I'd already been reading books and articles, watching podcasts and documentaries, trying to understand what trans was about. Nothing I learned reassured me. Instead I found out more and more about risks to health, long term damage to young and fragile bodies, changes that could not be undone and which would leave permanent scars – physical and emotional.

What was it like for Samson? He had been given a great gift – mighty strength. On the battlefield, he slaughtered his enemies. He had no fear, for the power of God was in him. In a time when the people of Israel lived with the constant threat of Philistine raiders stealing their hard work and effort – their crops and livestock, Samson lived to defend his people against attack. And then as the result of one foolish revelation, it was all taken away. His hair was cut off, his head shaved, and the Holy Spirit withdrew from him. Samson's freedom was taken away with his power. His sight was cruelly gouged out. Heavy shackles restricting his movement, rubbing his skin raw as he was forced to work for his enemy.

I cannot know what you are going through, the pain you are experiencing, the sense of loss, the level of fear, the grief or despair. I hadn't realised until it happened what the loss of my children would do to me. Estrangement is a weapon and a defence used by the trans identifying child to force parents and others to accommodate and even celebrate their identity, to shield them from the uncomfortable truth – that their parents know who they really are. When a child declares they are trans, some parents feel compelled to go along with it. I now have much more sympathy with those parents who desperately try anything to maintain connection with the trans identifying child. I have been devastated by estrangement.

Yet we are parents, not hostages, not prisoners. We have been given a responsibility by God to raise our children. This God given responsibility comes with power and authority. If you read through the book of Genesis, you find fathers who bless their children. This was prophetic – a miraculous gift from God. I should not assume that just because I ask God something for my child that it will happen. Yet Jesus told us to ask, and to seek, and to keep knocking on Heaven's door. We can influence what happens through our relationship with our Father in Heaven. Our children have free will, though when their will has been deceived and corrupted as I believe so many of our children have by trans ideology, their will is not their own. Should we not pray that they will be set free? That the shackles that bind them be broken off?

You may have been through a time of great despair, you may be about to enter that valley of the shadow of death. If you feel your power has been taken away, your hope, your joy, your life, let your hair grow back in. God uses time to heal us. Hair grows back in slowly, gradually. We do not notice it growing, and yet after a few days, stubble has appeared. Give it a few weeks and our head is noticeably covered once more. If you are familiar with the story of Samson, the writer seems to indicate that as his hair grew back in, the power of God was once again restored to him. Having been humbled, Samson finally prayed for God to strengthen him once more and God answered his prayer. Ask God to give you your strength back. Be patient as he does this. You may not notice it happening, yet God continues to work in your life.

> *Do not despise these small beginnings,*
> *for the Lord rejoices to see the work begin,*
> *to see the plumb line in Zerubbabel's hand."*
> *Zechariah 4:10*

We say time is a great healer. The truth is that God created time, gifted us with time. Time to heal, time to renew our strength, time for our faith to increase again.

Allow God to work in you and you will find God works through you again.

Father in Heaven, thank you that you have not given up on us. You have not abandoned us and left us to despair. You care about our child, our children and us. You love us more than we can ever know. Bless you that even now, you care what happens to our child. Father, please help us to learn patience. To trust in you through this time. Fill us with your power again, fill us with your Holy Spirit. Restore our strength and help us to seek this restoration from you. You are the source of our power, the source of our very life. May we see your power at work in us and through us once more. Amen

Day 3 — I will not lie, unless...

> *The king of Jericho was told, "Look, some of the Israelites have come here tonight to spy out the land." So the king of Jericho sent this message to Rahab: "Bring out the men who came to you and entered your house, because they have come to spy out the whole land."*
> *But the woman had taken the two men and hidden them. She said, "Yes, the men came to me, but I did not know where they had come from. At dusk, when it was time to close the city gate, they left. I don't know which way they went. Go after them quickly. You may catch up with them." (But she had taken them up to the roof and hidden them under the stalks of flax she had laid out on the roof.)*
> *So the men set out in pursuit of the spies on the road that leads to the fords of the Jordan, and as soon as the pursuers had gone out, the gate was shut.*
> *Joshua 2:2-7*

I was taught as a child that I should not lie. Wasn't this the ninth commandment? Not quite:

> *"You shall not give false testimony against your neighbour."*
> *Exodus 20:16*

False testimony is indeed a lie, but a lie may not be false testimony against one's neighbour. Most of us have heard stories of those saved by those willing to lie. As a child I heard again and again the stories of Anne Frank and Corrie Ten Boom. Tens of thousands of Jews were spared for a time by those willing to lie to the Nazis, and some were ultimately saved from the concentration camps because people bore false testimony for their Jewish neighbours, not against them. Likewise in the account from Joshua, we find Rahab using false testimony to save the Jewish spies.

I swore to myself that I would not lie to my child when I found out they identified as trans. Yet you could argue I did – by using my child's new name and even at one point the pronouns they asked me to. I tried to justify my use of my child's new name and preferred pronouns by being open and honest about the fact I was experimenting with it. Trying it out. I was aware that a child who refuses all contact with their parents is a child who is isolated. If there is communication, there may be influence. And if not influence, there may at least be the chance to show the child they are still loved and the door is open when they finally feel the need to return home.

I wanted the chance of communication, a conversation where I could try to understand what my child wanted, why my child wanted that. I wanted to see if there was room to compromise. Compromise is not always bad, not always evil, though sometimes it is.

I've spoken to many parents and read the stories of others. We each are trying to find a way to maintain relationships while not encouraging or affirming the harmful lies our children have accepted. For some this compromise involves choosing to use a new name and pronouns having made clear the parent does not believe in the new identity. Of course a risk with doing this is that the parent can become confused over time. What we say influences what we think. Some parents can hold that tension, while others cannot. There also appears to be a risk that by using the child's preferred name and pronouns that this may enforce their false beliefs about themselves. Teenagers may need us to resist them as they are testing their boundaries, and it is more healthy for them to know where the limits of their behaviour is than for us to agree there are no limits.

Rahab lied to protect the Israeli spies because she knew God was with them, that her people were afraid, and she wanted to save her own life and that of her family. In doing so, she risked her own life as she would surely have been put to death had the King discovered her deception.

Each family is different. Your situation is not mine. Your child has needs mine does not have and vice versa. We need the wisdom of God to guide us. Words of knowledge from the Holy Spirit. Our fight is not against flesh and blood, but principalities and powers – how true that statement is! May God give you the wisdom you need to know what to say and when to say it. When even a lie might be justified for the sake of your child's future and when only the truth will do.

Father in heaven, please, give us your wisdom, the guidance of your Holy Spirit. Lead us through this dark and dangerous journey. Shine your light on our family, on our children's lives and on our own. Expose what needs to be exposed. Help us to know when we must speak the truth to our children, and when we need to compromise. Lead our children back to us that we might be able to show them we love them. Allow us to have Godly influence over our children. Convict and forgive us when we have spoken wrong, and assure us when we have your blessing. Deliver us from the lies of the evil one who would make us doubt we have been led by you. Amen

Day 4 — Be strong in the Lord

> *Finally, be strong in the Lord and in his mighty power. Put on the full armour of God, so that you can take your stand against the devil's schemes. For our struggle is not against flesh and blood, but against the rulers, against the authorities, against the powers of this dark world and against the spiritual forces of evil in the heavenly realms. Therefore put on the full armour of God, so that when the day of evil comes, you may be able to stand your ground, and after you have done everything, to stand.*
> *Ephesians 6:10-13*

At times I have tried to take a stand against whatever spiritual forces of evil have a hold of my child. It has not taken long before I have fallen, confused and defeated. Why does my prayer for my child seem to have little or no effect? My child has free will, of course. I believe each of us can resist God, and God will not force us to bend our will. Not usually anyway. Though God did pursue Jonah, and perhaps that would be worth meditating on, and praying through.

I would love to be able to write about the above passage with authority and give you clear guidance. The truth is, I don't know if I have failed the test, or am still sitting it, perhaps for the hundredth time. I am reminded though of the many movies and TV shows where the weak man is knocked down, and despite all reason to stay down, still he struggles back up, first to a knee, then to his feet. Perhaps I am drawn to such characters because I can relate so well to them. Am I not always finding myself struggling once again to stand after being knocked down. I believe that for many of us, this is what we face as our child identifies as trans. A series of attacks and blows that humble us and threaten to cripple us. Our world, our beliefs, our reality is assaulted. For some it is too much. The threat of losing one's child is too severe. That loss would be more than we could bear. Some people succumb, give in. Go along with the lie until the lie almost seems to be the truth. That seems to be an extremely fragile reality, where no doubt can be entertained as it endangers the whole shaky edifice. If you have moved house and accepted a lie as your foundation, how could you bear to examine that foundation? Would you not be filled with utter terror at the void you are in danger of falling into? Could you ever bring yourself to ask: what have I done?

Those who do ask, those who investigate and expose their actions and beliefs to the bright and piercing light of Jesus Christ, they find the hand of God held out to them, offering rescue. Offering salvation.

In his letter, Paul does not tell the Ephesian church to be strong in themselves, or in their own power. No, they were told as we must be told – it is in the Lord that we are to be strong, and in his mighty power. I am weak, but he is strong. So, each day, perhaps multiple times each day, I must return to the source of power, to the source of strength. I do not need to do this on my own. You are not alone. Each of us can draw on the strength and power of our Father in heaven, in our Lord and Saviour, Jesus Christ.

We are told so little about these spiritual forces of evil. They are hinted at, alluded to such as in this account by Daniel:

Day 4: Be strong in the Lord

__Then he continued, "Do not be afraid, Daniel. Since the first day that you set your mind to gain understanding and to humble yourself before your God, your words were heard, and I have come in response to them. But the prince of the Persian kingdom resisted me twenty-one days. Then Michael, one of the chief princes, came to help me, because I was detained there with the king of Persia."__
__Daniel 10:12-13__

The prince of the Persian kingdom resisted the messenger sent by God to Daniel for three weeks. The three weeks Daniel had been mourning and fasting after he had received a revelation of the end times. Daniel was a man who prayed. A man who sought God. His whole life was dedicated to honouring and serving God. As a result, his enemies tried to have Daniel killed. And even though Daniel prayed and fasted, we are clearly told that sometimes the answers he sought were a long time coming. Perhaps three weeks of mourning does not seem all that big a deal. I am reminded of Joseph – seemingly abandoned in prison for two years, his only chance of rescue content to forget about him. Yet I believe Joseph continued to faithfully serve. Can I state without doubt that Joseph had faith throughout those long years in prison? No. He may well have doubted, may well have despaired. Yet throughout that time, no matter how many times he was knocked down, he managed to cling onto his God such that when he finally was brought before Pharaoh, he faithfully acknowledged it was God alone who gave the interpretation to Pharaohs dreams.

This journey we are on, as parents of children identifying as trans, we do not know how long it will be. Months? Years? A lifetime? This may be a long day of evil.

To stand against this, we need the power of God, the strength of our Lord Jesus Christ.

Father in heaven, I acknowledge and confess I need your strength, I need your power in my life. I am in despair. I am bereft. I cannot see a way out. But you know the end from the beginning. You have seen what will be. You know my child's future, and you care about my child far more than I do or can. Strengthen me to take my stand against this day of evil. May I stand rooted firmly in your word, in your power and in your strength. I need you. Each and every day I need you. Father, be my strength, and may I see my child saved and brought back to you, and brought back to me. Amen

Day 5

A time to mourn

*There is a time for everything,
and a season for every activity
under the heavens:
Ecclesiastes 3:1*

We are in mourning, many of us, parents of trans identified children who have killed off their former selves, buried the child we loved so dearly, and denied us the right to grieve. Dead Naming is what they accuse us of if we show any sign of mourning their former identity. As if our child is dead and a stranger stands in their place. For some of us, we are denied even that conflict, that struggle of deciding whether to affirm the new identity and attempt to forget the old, or resisting and dealing with the wrath such a choice often provokes. For those of us who are estranged from our child we may be able to mourn in private, knowing there may still be a cost to publicly declaring our grief.

Ecclesiastes begins with this statement that perhaps many parents in our situation can identify with:

*"Meaningless! Meaningless!"
says the Teacher.
"Utterly meaningless!
Everything is meaningless."
Ecclesiastes 1:2*

When a child can change their gender at will, embark on a journey of self-harm, and almost everyone in authority appears to encourage and celebrate this, can there be any meaning left in the world? These are cliches, yet they seem important to use: the rug is pulled from under your feet. Your world is shaken. Your child is no more and yet your child is right there! You are maybe looking at them, trying to comprehend a nonsense, to understand an insanity. It can drive us mad.

> *...a time to weep and a time to laugh,*
> *a time to mourn and a time to dance...*
> *Ecclesiastes 3:4*

I have laughed, frequently over the last two and half years, laughed at the insanity of it all. There has not been much dancing. There has been a lot of weeping and a fair amount of mourning.

Give yourself permission to mourn. Your child may be alive, may be in your face each and every day demanding you submit, bow down to their instruction, worship their new religion. Having been estranged, I cannot know how difficult that must be, and perhaps this day is not for you, this meditation on mourning. If so, feel free to move onto the next day and return if and when you are drawn back.

Psychiatrist Elisabeth Kübler-Ross is said to have recognised five stages of grief:

- Denial
- Anger
- Bargaining
- Depression
- Acceptance

I am no psychiatrist or psychologist so please bear in

mind I am simply sharing what I've experienced, observed or read about. I have joked that upon being told of my child's new trans identity I did a full Homer Simpson, without the donut. If you've not seen that episode of the Simpson's, on being told he is going to die, in the space of around 30 seconds, Homer displays each of the above five stages.

It took me a lot longer than 30 seconds and in reality I spiralled and have continued to spiral through these stages ever since. While the five stages sound clean and distinct, grief and mourning is messy and confused. We may be experiencing denial while noticing depression or anger. May be unaware of our anger or depression thinking we have accepted the situation. Like a ball bearing in a pin ball machine we may suddenly bounce off of one stage onto another then rapidly to another. It may be a comfort to remember Jesus' reaction to seeing the grave of his friend, Lazarus:

> ***When Jesus saw her weeping, and the Jews who had come along with her also weeping, he was deeply moved in spirit and troubled. "Where have you laid him?" he asked.***
> ***"Come and see, Lord," they replied.***
> ***Jesus wept.***
> ***Then the Jews said,***
> ***"See how he loved him!"***
> ***John 11:33-36***

It is normal and acceptable to mourn the loss of a child. Some say that the death of a child is the worst thing a parent can experience. The fact that our child may still be very much alive does complicate things for us. Yet grief is also a normal and acceptable response to any situation which shatters our lives. We mourn for the loss of our child when they move out of our house, perhaps to go to college or university. We mourn for the loss when they get married. This does not mean that we do not also want them to become independent and find a faithful companion, yet it is common for parents to feel loss at such events. When our child rejects their very identity and threatens to harm themselves, on top of fear and anxiety and confusion, we may well feel loss. Loss of control. Loss of a sense of safety. Loss ultimately of our child, of our hopes and dreams for them. At such a time, it may be healthy for us to mourn that loss, to allow ourselves to grieve.

Father in heaven, you know what it is to mourn. Jesus' grief for his friend Lazarus shows us a measure of your grief, yet did you not also mourn when Adam and Eve turned away from you, when the good world you gave us was corrupted and cursed? Have you not also mourned since then for everyone who has died unnecessarily, for the pain and suffering caused by our sin? Thank you that you sent your son to heal and forgive. Thank you for Jesus, that you loved this world so much that you sent your son. Help us when the time is right to grieve for our child, to mourn for them and for ourselves. Guide us through our grief. Help us to express what we are feeling. Comfort us and heal us and give us strength to hold on for our child's future. To allow ourselves to mourn now so that one day we might dance and laugh when we see our child restored to you and to us. Amen

Day 6 — Speaking the truth

When we put bits into the mouths of horses to make them obey us, we can turn the whole animal. Or take ships as an example. Although they are so large and are driven by strong winds, they are steered by a very small rudder wherever the pilot wants to go. Likewise, the tongue is a small part of the body, but it makes great boasts. Consider what a great forest is set on fire by a small spark. The tongue also is a fire, a world of evil among the parts of the body.
It corrupts the whole body,
sets the whole course of one's life on fire,
and is itself set on fire by hell.
James 3:3-6

Today, when I came to write, I felt convicted. For a long time now I have told people that I am estranged from my children. My children do not want to see me or speak with me. Some who are in a similar situation may not be comfortable sharing something so personal. I certainly have strong feelings of guilt and shame over the breakdown in my relationship with my children. I have regrets over things I have said to them in the past, my words having hurt them. Some may prefer to avoid speaking about their children to avoid people judging them. At times I have done this, put on a mask, said my children are doing okay, thank you for asking. At other times I felt compelled to admit I was estranged as this was my perception of the situation. Is this an autistic trait in myself, that if I believe something to be true, I find myself wanting to say it, even though in our culture – to be estranged from one's children stigmatises the parent? Would it not be easier to just tell a white lie? Sometimes we must be careful who we entrust with the truth. Not everyone means us well. Some people do gossip. Others may use the truth against us.

But was it true that I was estranged from my children? Did I make it true through repeated statements?

I do not subscribe to the belief that what we say will be done for us. The "Universe" doesn't owe us anything. There is no "Secret" that enables some to speak prosperity into their lives. Yet God's word does caution us in many places to use our words carefully. James' letter is just one which contains several instructions about the importance of speech. In Romans 12, Paul writes we are to bless and not curse. Peter also gives the same advice in 1 Peter 3.

Was I speaking a curse over my life when I said "I am estranged from my children"? Curses do have some power. Sometimes a lot of power. Just as blessings also can have some power or a lot of power.

So, am I estranged from my children or not? All of my children have avoided me for a long time. My trans identifying child has refused to speak with me for two and a half years. Yet, in the words I speak, do I want to submit to this situation, or speak words of blessing into it? Will God honour me when I say "I am estranged from my children"? Perhaps. Perhaps God will hear me saying those words and say, well, if these are the words he speaks over himself – he can have that. I find that a scary thought. That I could inadvertently curse myself. And even if it is not that God would give us what we speak over our lives, might it be that we will come to believe what we say of ourselves, and so act as if it was true when if we had spoken blessing, we might have acted as if the blessing was true and so brought about a change for the better?

I had a conviction today, that I need to stop saying "I am estranged" and find something more positive to say. Something that I want God to honour and bless me with. Something that might encourage me to act in a way that helps to heal the relationship. What to say though when someone asks about my children? How to convey the grief I feel, or the anger, or the sense of loss or frustration? Or do I need to share any of that?

If someone asks me – "How are your children?" – a common question. A natural question to a parent. How can I answer, maintaining my integrity while also speaking blessing over our relationship? Perhaps I could say this: "I haven't heard from my children in a while," – that is the truth as I write – "and I pray our relationship will be restored soon." – I speak blessing over the relationship.

It will be good for me to consider some scenarios. Common questions I might be asked, and prepare some responses so I am ready to speak words of blessing, rather than being caught off guard and saying the first thing that comes to mind. Though if I speak something I immediately regret, I can then correct myself. I can admit that I did not want to say that. I can even say I should not have said that, and instead choose to say something that is a blessing. This will take discipline on our part and it would be good to consider how James continues in his teaching:

With the tongue we praise our Lord and Father, and with it we curse human beings, who have been made in God's likeness. Out of the same mouth come praise and cursing. My brothers and sisters, this should not be. Can both fresh water and salt water flow from the same spring? My brothers and sisters, can a fig tree

bear olives, or a grapevine bear figs? Neither can a salt spring produce fresh water.
James 3:9-12

The tongue can be a world of evil. It can also be used to bless and to praise God. Whatever our tongues say, whatever comes out of our mouth, it has it's source in our heart. Will I, will we allow love for our children to overcome the despair we might feel? Will we let Jesus in to calm our troubled thoughts? Will we allow his Holy Spirit to comfort us in our grief? Will we surrender any anger we feel to him and speak the truth over our children – that Jesus has a plan for our child's life, that Jesus loves our child, that Jesus is calling our child back to him. May the kindness of Jesus lead our child away from danger and towards life.

Father in heaven, thank you that you warn us about the consequences of what we say. Your words brought our world into being. Your words brought life in the form of your Son, Jesus. Your words brought salvation through Jesus to save us from our sin. Where I have spoken words that were a curse, where I inadvertently speak these words in future, Father through your Holy Spirit, convict me. Teach me to speak words of blessing over my children, over my relationship with them. And may my relationship with my children be restored. May hurt and wounds and pain that they and I feel all be healed. Amen

Day 7

Shall I pursue them?

When David and his men reached Ziklag, they found it destroyed by fire and their wives and sons and daughters taken captive. So David and his men wept aloud until they had no strength left to weep. David's two wives had been captured – Ahinoam of Jezreel and Abigail, the widow of Nabal of Carmel. David was greatly distressed because the men were talking of stoning him; each one was bitter in spirit because of his sons and daughters. But David found strength in the Lord his God.
Then David said to Abiathar the priest, the son of Ahimelek, 'Bring me the ephod.' Abiathar brought it to him, and David enquired of the Lord, 'Shall I pursue this raiding party? Will I overtake them?' 'Pursue them,' he answered. 'You will certainly overtake them and succeed in the rescue.'
1 Samuel 30:3-8

When I was first told that my child – who had by this point run away from home – identified as trans, one of my first thoughts was to go to her. I imagined myself camping outside the house where she was staying, perhaps holding a sign telling her I loved her, a statement she could not ignore. I contemplated taking her – by force if necessary – and returning her home where we could help her. Different scenarios went through my mind. I wanted to play the hero, to save my child from disaster. I asked God what to do but did not receive any clear direction. I can't recall now if I had recently read some articles on rescuing people from cults. Whether it was before or during those early days I cannot recall and yet I did read them and found myself influenced by what I'd read. The advice given was that a person is rarely rescued from a cult, instead they must make the decision to leave all by themselves. If they are taken out of the cult, in many cases, the person will try to return.

My child had already run away from home. It was only slowly that I came to realise this. I found evidence that she had been planning to leave for some time and over weeks and months, the evidence grew that she had chosen to run away. She was now staying with family members and so we were glad she was relatively safe. I say relatively as the fear she planned to take experimental drugs and submit to surgery was terrifying to me. It was communicated to us that she was well. We got some news occasionally. The longer it went on, the more confused I became. Should I go to her, should I attempt to talk with her, should I write to her? I did write and even sent some of those letters over a period of months. Until very recently I did not know if she ever read any of them. A Zoom call was arranged and we attempted to talk to her, but she left the room without saying a word.

As I write this, it has been over two and a half years. I still don't know if my restraining myself was the right thing for my child, or if it would have been better to go to her at the very beginning, even to insist she return home with us.

There were other circumstances. Family members who were opposed to us and made it very clear the situation was out of our hands. A Government who was supportive of trans ideology and many stories of parents losing their fight to protect their children.

I cannot say I heard from God. I cannot even be sure I was really listening for an answer to the many questions I asked of God. But that is not totally true. We had some answers to prayer, probably even a lot of answers from God. Situations that were reversed. Lines of communication opened. Protection in bad situations. Still though, I look back and wonder – should I have pursued her?

In some ways it seems David had it easy. His wives and children and the wives and children of his men had all been taken. He asked God what to do and God said – go, you will succeed and rescue your family. But the account of the situation is brief and only highlights a few things. David feared for his life. He was at risk of his men turning on him and killing him. And of course when he overtook the raiding party that had taken the wives and children, then David had to fight. He had to fight and kill and keep on fighting and killing until there was no more danger. It is so easy from my office chair to dismiss such a situation, to gloss over it. David and his men had to go to war. David would have led his men into battle risking his life from the minute they charged to the moment the last of their enemies was killed.

Even now I am asking myself – should I pursue them – my children, each of whom has been estranged from us for so, so long; or would it push them further away? I do believe this account of David seeking God is important to us parents. David sought the guidance of God and God advised him. God will advise us as well. Though sometimes we will have to keep pursuing God for an answer.

I recall the science fiction series I read as a teenager: *Foundation* – by Isaac Asimov. A novel that was so strange for almost nothing happening. Crises were anticipated and in each case the leaders recognised they were to respond to the specific crisis by doing nothing.

In some cases – this is what God wants us to do. He will fight the fight. He will overcome the enemy. He will drive our enemies out before us, send them into confusion, blind them, make them fight amongst themselves. All we have to do is listen to God, be obedient to him, and we will see victory.

At other times though, God will give us a different answer. He will instruct us to go, pursue, and to fight. Which answer will God give to you in the situation you find yourself? Only God has the answer.

As for me, perhaps I received no answer in order that I could share this story with you. Perhaps if God had given me clear direction, I would have foolishly thought that I should advise everyone I met to do the same. Instead, I have been left with uncertainty, and in that uncertainty I have had to keep seeking God. And Jesus certainly had a few things to say about persistence in prayer.

Then Jesus told his disciples a parable to show them that they should always pray and not give up. He said:

"In a certain town there was a judge who neither feared God nor cared what people thought. And there was a widow in that town who kept coming to him with the plea, 'Grant me justice against my adversary.'

"For some time he refused. But finally he said to himself, 'Even though I don't fear God or care what people think, yet because this widow keeps bothering me, I will see that she gets justice, so that she won't eventually come and attack me!'"

And the Lord said, "Listen to what the unjust judge says. And will not God bring about justice for his chosen ones, who cry out to him day and night? Will he keep putting them off? I tell you, he will see that they get justice, and quickly. However, when the Son

of Man comes, will he find faith on the earth?"
Luke 18:1-8

If we do not get an answer as to what God would have us do, Jesus would have us keep praying, keep asking, keep seeking. And then the question becomes, when Jesus comes to us with the answer, will Jesus find us still listening, still pursuing him with faith in our hearts?

Father in heaven, you know exactly what we are going through as we are all your children and so many of us have been taken by strange cults, led astray to follow false gods and idols. You know the end from the beginning, what will be and whether our effort will succeed or fail. Please, Father, give us the answer to the question we ask. Should we pursue our children? Will we overtake them on the road they are on? Will we be able to persuade them to leave behind their captors and return with us? Will expressions of love make a difference or are we just casting pearls before swine? We love our children, and we know that you love us. But you set before us a choice and offer us options. You do not force any of us to follow you or love you and we cannot do that to our children either. Guide us and give us your wisdom. Amen

Day 8   A marathon not a sprint

If you point these things out to the brothers and sisters, you will be a good minister of Christ Jesus, nourished on the truths of the faith and of the good teaching that you have followed. Have nothing to do with godless myths and old wives' tales; rather, train yourself to be godly. For physical training is of some value, but godliness has value for all things, holding promise for both the present life and the life to come. This is a trustworthy saying that deserves full acceptance. That is why we labour and strive, because we have put our hope in the living God,
who is the Savior of all people,
and especially of those who believe.
1 Timothy 4:6-10

I want to disagree with Paul. A dangerous thing to do I know. In his letter to Timothy, Paul writes that physical training is of some value. My disagreement is simply that exercise has a lot of value, especially for those of us who hold office jobs, or live such lives that give our physical body no regular workout.

Paul lived in a time when almost everyone would have worked hard. Even obtaining water to drink, cook or wash with may have required immense effort. Even at the height of Roman civilisation, for most people, live was difficult. They would have walked everywhere putting our need for step counters to shame. Perhaps the very rich with their slaves and servants would have lived lives more resembling ours. Ordering take-aways online and barely managing to walk to the door to receive one's meal might not be too far removed from the master of the house commanding a meal be prepared and brought to him or her.

Gluttony was a problem in Paul's day. Even his instruction on the Lord's Supper in his first letter to the Corinthian church (see chapter 11) made reference to those who ate with no regard for their poorer brothers and sisters. The good news of Jesus Christ is for the poor, though in our messed-up civilisation, some who are poor are obese, and some who work cannot afford to feed themselves.

Paul wants his readers to understand that godliness has value for all things, and this is true. I would agree with anyone who argued that we should pursue godliness, indeed my first 31 Days of Prayer book explored turning away from an ungodly life to a godly one. In later days I'll be looking at the armour of God and working through what relevance this has to us as parents. Yet in our situation – those of us with trans identifying children, exercise – physical training – likely also has great value.

When I first heard my child identified as trans, I was already aware that some children remain trapped in that belief for many years. I had heard stories of parents having to contend with the situation for six years, eight years, a decade. I could not cope with that knowledge. Truly, Jesus said:

"Therefore do not worry about tomorrow, for tomorrow will worry about itself. Each day has enough trouble of its own."
Matthew 6:34

Yet, while our trouble continues and it will be better for our mental health if we do not catastrophise about the future, it likely will also benefit us through this trial, this ordeal, if we act like we are in a marathon, rather than burning ourselves out in the assumption this is a sprint and it will all be over soon.

My mental health is better for regular exercise. In those early days after we were told about our child, my wife and I went for walks every day that we could. Even getting out of the house when it is pouring with rain lifts my spirit. When I wrote Double Your Salary, I focused on three goals that seemed to have a harmonic resonance, each goal benefiting another: writing a novel, pursuing a career, and studying for a degree. Not too long after I published Double Your Salary I remembered there was a fourth goal that had often also contributed to that harmonic resonance: exercise. I had set exercise goals at different stages. To attend the gym twice a week; to run a 10k; learn to climb. I did not maintain any of the goals longer term. After I ran the 10k, my running dropped off. I no longer climb. Yet I can recall the benefit those activities gave me. At the start of this year (2024) I did restart attending a gym and am managing to go at least twice a week. It is helping me.

I have a job that requires me to sit in a chair for eight hours a day. That is not good for my physical or mental health. Combine this with fear and grief for my child, possible undiagnosed depression, and if I made no effort at physical training, I likely would be in a worse state than I currently am.

I do not know your personal situation. Perhaps you have a physical job and so have no need to attend a gym. Maybe you already walk for miles and miles each day and manage to get outside and benefit from the sun and the boost that being outdoors gives us. If so – carry on doing what you are doing! Physical exercise has a benefit. If we are in this for the long term, if we are in a marathon that we did not choose but was forced on us, looking after our physical health will have a positive impact on our mental and emotional health. And if we can find some exercise or activity that our child will want to do with us – so much the better! I was not able to do this, but some parents have found outdoor activities, or sports that they and their child can participate in. If not, then at least look after yourself. Physical training is of immense value to those of us in this for the long haul. Do pray for a miracle, but prepare for a marathon.

Father in heaven, give us wisdom to see what we need to do to maintain and improve our physical and mental and emotional health. Where we are weak, where we are out of shape, help us to make a start, to do one thing each day to build our strength and resilience. You gave us these bodies to use, to dance and jump and run – may we glorify you and enjoy the gift of being active. Strengthen our weak knees. Empower us to exercise. Help us to discipline ourselves. Help us to give our troubles to you, to trust in you each day, and yet also live each day in such a way that we can continue, that we can maintain our pace over the time we have to face our trial. Amen

Day 9 — When your hopes are dashed

Not only so, but we also glory in our sufferings, because we know that suffering produces perseverance; perseverance, character; and character, hope. And hope does not put us to shame, because God's love has been poured out into our hearts through the Holy Spirit, who has been given to us.
Romans 5:3-5

I am writing this book while I am still on this terrible journey. At some point in the past did I ask God for an adventure? Maybe. It is the sort of thing I likely would have done. You know the problem with adventures, right? Those who go off on an adventure face trials and peril and danger. Welcome to the Christian life! Suffering is a feature, not a bug.

Over the past weeks I'd thought there was thawing of my relationship with one of my older children. We'd had a phone call. Not just a quick two-minute call, but an extended one where they had shared what was happening in their life, filling us in on experiences at work, their studies, and their plans for the immediate future. We'd exchanged texts. My child had responded to my messages, replying instead of seeming to ignore them. They shared they had a need, and I'd sent money. It seemed like maybe our child wanted us back in their life. I suggested meeting up. They told us that they had an opportunity to work in another city in the South of England. I'd offered help with the move, suggesting we hire a car and could share the driving. I began to look forward to some real face to face time with my child.

Yesterday I got a phone call. My child didn't want to see me. Didn't want my help with the move. I had got my hopes up. Hoped to spend some time with them and they were too busy. Too focused on what they had to do, and perhaps they have inherited my autistic traits which prevent me from seeing what is most important until after it is too late. I never learned the lesson of that song: Cat's in the cradle. Now I am seeing my child follow my example: focused on work and career. My hopes of a chance to reconcile, to listen, to have time to ask questions, all my hopes were dashed.

On this terrible journey we parents of trans identified children are on, there may be many times when our hopes are dashed. We are not promised an easy life. We are promised suffering. We are also promised that through suffering our character will be developed.

I don't know how to glory in my sufferings, but as I was thinking about all this this morning, I recalled other times when people suffered. In the final chapter of 2 Chronicles, we are told of the end of Israel. Nebuchadnezzar conquers Jerusalem and carries off all the articles from the Temple, slaughters most of the people and carries off as prisoners a remnant to become his slaves. Their hopes were dashed. What must it have been like to have been taken prisoner in this way? Perhaps your parents killed in front of you, your brothers, sisters, friends. All whom you love. And where was God in all this? Well, we know where God was – he had been warning Israel of this danger for Centuries. It had been prophesied by Moses that the consequence of them turning away from God was disaster and destruction. Moses even wrote his own Cat's in the cradle song in Deuteronomy 32. Yet despite all this suffering, the book of 2 Chronicles gives a hint of hope:

Day 9: When your hopes are dashed

> ***The land enjoyed its sabbath rests; all the time of its desolation it rested, until the seventy years were completed in fulfilment of the word of the Lord spoken by Jeremiah.***
> ***2 chronicles 36:21***

Seventy years. That is a lifetime, a literal lifetime. It was likely that not one person taken into captivity in Babylon would live to see Jerusalem restored. Will we live to see our child redeemed? I cannot say. Yet I can say that there were those who persevered through that terrible time. The book of Daniel records the actions of four men, Daniel included. Those who chose to serve their God despite the risk to their own lives. Who loved God with all their heart and soul and mind and strength. They persevered through the suffering. And as they persevered, their character developed. And they saw the most amazing miracles. I cannot say that I or you will see the sort of miracle for our children that those men saw: saved from the fire or the lions, yet perhaps we will see the sort of miracle Paul spoke of, that if we can continue to put our hope in God, can trust in him through our suffering, then God's love will be poured into us and through us, by his Holy Spirit. That we will be able to persevere. That our character will be developed such that even if our hopes for our children are repeatedly dashed, that we will not give up hoping in God and maybe that will be miracle enough. Yet I express my hope that in the end, however long it takes, our prayers for our children will be answered and one day they will return to God and to us and as the Israelites eventually rejoiced as they returned to Jerusalem, so we will rejoice at the return of our children.

Father in heaven, I am in despair. I do not know how long I can go on. I feel like giving up. In fact, you must have heard me say it: I give up! But Father, let me give it up to you. Let me give up my fears and grief and despair all to you. I give my child to you. I cannot, but you can. Father, please lead my child back to you. Call them and direct them. Convict them and let them know they are judged by you. Lead them to repentance and into your mercy and grace. Deliver my child from this false belief they are trans. Give them hope that they can have peace and contentment in their body, with you as their comfort. Amen

Day 10 — Am I a coward at heart?

As for those of you who are left, I will make their hearts so fearful in the lands of their enemies that the sound of a windblown leaf will put them to flight. They will run as though fleeing from the sword, and they will fall, even though no one is pursuing them. They will stumble over one another as though fleeing from the sword, even though no one is pursuing them. So you will not be able to stand before your enemies. You will perish among the nations; the land of your enemies will devour you. Those of you who are left will waste away in the lands of their enemies because of their sins; also because of their ancestors' sins they will waste away.
Leviticus 26:36-39

I fear I am a coward. I know I should speak up at work and in other environments when others make false claims about the need to affirm a child's trans identity. I believe that there is a need for more and more of us to speak publicly about what is true, to challenge the lies, the misuse of language such as preferred pronouns and dehumanising language like "birthing person". Yet when I attempt to do so, often my bowels feel like they might empty, my hands shake, my knees tremble. I am like an old man, a cowardly old man, too scared to put my head above the parapet in case I get shot.

I wrote an email, challenging the promotion of gender and trans identity through Pride and LGBTQ+. I've written earlier that others have already given ample evidence why such promotion is unhealthy and even dangerous. I recommend books and websites listed in the Resources section at the end of this book for anyone who has doubts and questions. The email I'd written was the fifth or sixth such email, none of the others sent. I started off so brave, but quickly was reduced once more to fear. I've had many people now tell me that to write such emails and not send them is a good way to process the thoughts I have. It is cathartic to write down my feelings. It is helpful to work through why I am feeling and thinking what I am. Yet each year, Pride month is celebrated in our pagan culture and each year it makes me sick to my stomach.

I've been reading through Leviticus. What a difficult book to read. I struggled and felt guilty and ashamed while reading it. Jesus may have fulfilled the law, yet does he not still call us to holiness, to being set apart from the people of this world? Yes, he does. And how are we to understand holiness or being set apart if we never go back to the law that Jesus fulfilled for us?

I wrote that email yesterday, not having yet read Leviticus 26. It is a chapter of contrasts. Of instruction and the laying out of the consequence of failing to follow the Lord's instruction. Like its parallel chapter in Deuteronomy 28, Moses recounts the rewards for obeying God and the punishment for disobeying God. Cowardice is a punishment. Bravery is a reward. Yet that may be too simplistic.

You will pursue your enemies, and they will fall by the sword before you. Five of you will chase a hundred, and a hundred of you will chase ten thousand, and your enemies will fall by the sword before you.
Leviticus 26:7-8

Day 10: Am I a coward at heart?

The reward here is not bravery, it is that ones' enemies will flee from us. I have a vague memory of a scene from a movie, of someone throwing caution to the wind and rising up and charging at the enemy, and the gathered enemies suddenly shocked, thrown off-guard, and in their confusion they are routed. It is not necessarily brave to charge at the enemy. So many soldiers in the first World War were ordered to do so despite being desperately afraid and rightly so. Though I acknowledge that true bravery is doing something important that one is afraid to do. Yet it is this contradiction I'm trying to understand. I was afraid while writing the email. Just an email. And also not just an email. An email that could have consequences for me. I've seen so many people suffer for speaking up. Contracts terminated. The blackening of names. Ridicule. The smearing of reputation such that people may not be able to find work again. Should we not fear such consequences? 'You will pursue your enemies'. It does not promise we will feel brave while doing so, only that our enemies will flee before us. At least, if we are being rewarded by God. And that is a big if!

And punishment for disobedience? If a punishment is that I will feel like and act like a coward, how do I tell whether or not I am being punished? I am concerned for other colleagues who are parents, concerned they may be being misled into harming their children. When I attempt to write a simple email challenging the promotion of gender affirmation, and I am terrified to do so, is that punishment or not? Well, earlier in Leviticus I had read this:

The Lord said to Moses, "The tenth day of this seventh month is the Day of Atonement. Hold a sacred assembly and deny yourselves, and present a

***food offering to the Lord. Do not do any work on that day, because it is the Day of Atonement, when atonement is made for you before the Lord your God.
Leviticus 23:26-28***

The Israelites were to set apart one day a year as a day of atonement. And deny themselves. Deny themselves what? It is likely they were expected to fast. To go a whole day without eating. That is certainly denying oneself. Given earlier commands it is also likely they were to refrain from sexual activity on that day. And it possibly, probably goes further than that. It was a day for the Israelites to humble themselves. To acknowledge their need for God, their need for forgiveness, their need for a saviour. Each and every sacrifice listed in Leviticus points to Jesus who atoned for our sin, our weakness, our failings. I feel it is not a coincidence that I was reading about the command to humble oneself during the secular celebration of Pride month. A whole month to celebrate Pride? What could be more at odds with the commands of God than that? God commands us to humble ourselves. And there is a reward promised for those who do humble themselves. Many rewards promised. We individually may not reap all those rewards since we live in societies that I believe are currently being punished for our worship of false idols and our disobedience to God. Yet as Abraham negotiated with the Lord for Sodom and that account shows us God will spare a city for the few righteous found there, it does not yet seem that we are all being punished as severely as we might.

I found myself praying a lot while writing that email. Acknowledging my need for God. Humbling myself in my heart. And also afterwards. And that seems important as well. For after I wrote the email, I managed to click send.

And almost instantly there was a temptation towards pride, towards an "I did this" attitude. A false bravado. But I did not manage to write and send that email alone, certainly not in my own strength. It was God who gave me courage. God who sustained me. God who guided me. I may have written the words, yet I asked the Holy Spirit to inspire me. And if my email failed on any level, that is on me. Yet if the email has an effect, if there is a positive result – then may God receive the praise! You cannot know how weak I was, how scared I was, how ready I was to simply file that email away in a folder that no-one would ever see. Or maybe you can because you are just like me. I need the strength of my God, the empowering of his Holy Spirit. We all do. May you be encouraged to speak the truth and to challenge lies when you hear them. If you feel fear when you are prompted to speak out, may you turn to your Father in heaven who is able to do all things.

Father in heaven, help each of us to humble ourselves before you, to acknowledge our need for you, especially when it comes to our children. May we humble ourselves to listen to your commands and examine our lives in the light of them. Where we have failed to obey you, to respect you, to honour you in our lives, may we repent, humbling ourselves in our hearts and our actions. May you have mercy on me and on our family. Give us your courage to speak and act against those who would harm our children. And cause those who seek to lie to our children to lose their courage. May our enemies in this battle stumble and flee. May we see you at work in our lives and in our workplaces and communities. Amen

Day 11 — Robbed of our children

If you remain hostile toward me and refuse to listen to me, I will multiply your afflictions seven times over, as your sins deserve. I will send wild animals against you, and they will rob you of your children, destroy your cattle and make you so few in number that your roads will be deserted.
Leviticus 26:21-22

The Pied Piper of Hamelin is a cautionary tale. Beware of breaking your contract with someone who has power that you do not have, they may turn against you. I'm sure you see why I refer to that legend though allow me to explore it today.

As well as rewards for obedience listed in Leviticus 26, there are punishments for disobedience listed. Wild animals who will rob us of our children – I can't help but connect this warning with what I see happening to our children today, and also to the legend of the Pied Piper.

In Scotland we have a trans identifying activist who likes to dress up in costume. A year or more ago I attended a rally: Let Women Speak in Glasgow's George Square. I felt it was important for me, a man, to turn up and listen. I foolishly thought I might even get a chance to speak myself, but it turned out there were dozens of women who wanted to speak, and hundreds more who turned out to listen. I was aware there was a protest rally taking place, organised by this activist, and part of me wondered if my daughter might be there, the counter protest claiming they were protecting the rights of people identifying as trans…

from women who wanted the right to speak. Not that my daughter may have wanted to stop women from speaking, simply that she may have wanted to join with others who identify as trans and been drawn to that counter protest. I had no idea what she may or may not have wanted. Being estranged my thoughts wander.

Anyway, I walked away from the Let Women Speak event and wandered over to the counter protest. I regret not taking some video now, though perhaps others did and shared it. What I saw was easily over a hundred young people, maybe even two hundred, surrounding this gaily dressed trans activist who was at the centre of these young people who had formed themselves into a conga line. Each with their hands on the person in front, snaking round and round this brightly coloured figure who looked to me just like a modern-day Pied Piper. Why would our children follow such a person? Some of them seem to feel misunderstood, or that they do not belong. Perhaps our child is in pain, and they have been convinced that their suffering can be eased and resolved by undergoing the transformation out of their biological sex and into the gender identity they perceive themselves to be. Slogans like "born in the wrong body" imply that their body and reality are lying to them. Where was this Pied Piper leading our children? Well, as I understand it, he was leading them away from their parents, robbing us of our children, leading them to a place where they could be sterilised, castrated, permanently harmed and disfigured by experimental drugs and hormones and surgeries. I cannot say that would be his understanding, but it was mine.

There is a slightly different figure from a more modern legend, that of the Child Catcher from the movie Chitty Chitty Bang Bang. I can't remember much else about that movie, but I do remember those scenes with the Child

Catcher. I watched those scenes as a child and found them disturbing then. As a parent now I remember and am horrified to realise that I have let my child be captured. How did that happen? How did I know of the danger and still manage to let my child be robbed away from me? How great must my sin have been that such a terrible event should happen. Except, what about Job? He was blameless we are told, and yet his children all were taken away from him. I feel that I should not assume too much either way. I am not Job that God would hold me up as someone blameless and upright. I am not solely responsible for the sin of society around me. I am responsible for my own failings as a father. I may also be punished for societies sin. Is that fair? Is that just? Who am I to argue with God? Who are you to judge God? We are warned there are consequences for disobeying God. We may not be the people of Israel, may not be subject to the law of Moses, yet we are all created by God, all people everywhere will one day have to give an account of our lives to Him. It does seem to me that we need to be aware that while we may be judged on our own lives and receive reward and/or punishment during our lives and in the Day of Judgement, we also benefit from living amongst people who serve God, and receive punishment from living among people who reject God. I am writing this book for parents who, like me, have been robbed of their children. I acknowledge my failings that have contributed to this and also acknowledge that at least in part, I have suffered this loss because my fellow citizens failed to humble themselves before their God, failed to give Him his due, and so we are being robbed of our children as a consequence. May God have mercy on us, mercy that we do not deserve. Mercy because of his great kindness. May our children be returned to both God and us.

Father in heaven, have mercy on us, sinners who live in a sinful land. I may deserve to be robbed of my children though I hate to think that. We may deserve to have our children robbed in our society today for turning away from you and rebelling against you. All I can do is humble myself before you, admit my sin, and beg for your forgiveness and mercy. Please Father, rescue my child. Deliver my child from those who have caught her and seduced her and led her away from both me and from you. Deliver our nation from this wickedness. Cause us to humble ourselves, to repent of our sin and turn back to you. Amen

Day 12 — Heroes in their own story

"But I did obey the Lord," Saul said. "I went on the mission the Lord assigned me. I completely destroyed the Amalekites and brought back Agag their king. The soldiers took sheep and cattle from the plunder, the best of what was devoted to God, in order to sacrifice them to the Lord your God at Gilgal."
But Samuel replied: "Does the Lord delight in burnt offerings and sacrifices as much as in obeying the Lord? To obey is better than sacrifice, and to heed is better than the fat of rams. For rebellion is like the sin of divination, and arrogance like the evil of idolatry. Because you have rejected the word of the Lord, he has rejected you as king."
1 Samuel 15:20-23

King Saul thought of himself as a hero. Anointed as the first king over Israel it seems from the account in 1 Samuel that he became proud even building a monument to himself after his perceived victory in battle. When challenged by the Lord's prophet Samuel, Saul protests, unable to accept his actions were not heroic. I find myself sympathising with Saul as I read. He made a mistake. I make mistakes. He was disobedient. I am disobedient. In a single moment, the kingdom was taken away from Saul and if you read on, even though Saul appears to confess his sin, it is too late, the hero king will not be forgiven.

This rejection of Saul is often contrasted with God's willingness to forgive the king who replaced him: David. What was it about Saul's sin that God could not forgive?

What was it about David's sin that God was willing to accept his repentance?

Saul disobeyed a direct command of God. When challenged, Saul tried to justify himself. When punished, Saul begged. He blamed the people stating he was afraid of them and showing he was not fit to be king. He would not accept God's punishment and so the punishment was increased.

David in contrast humbled himself in his confession – you can read the account in 2 Samuel 12. There was no justification, no begging, no blaming of other people. Yes, David did fast and pray for his son who was devoted by God for death, yet after the child died, David humbly accepted the situation. The contrast between Saul's inability to obey God and accept God's judgement with David's ability to do both is striking. And David's humility, his obedience earned him a place in history as a man after God's own heart:

After removing Saul, he made David their king. God testified concerning him: 'I have found David son of Jesse, a man after my own heart; he will do everything I want him to do.'
Acts 13:22

Everyone is a hero in their own story. None of us see ourselves as villains. As you go through life you've seen people hurt you and hurt others and now they are hurting your child, affirming your child in a lie. And they think they are the heroes. In their eyes, what they are doing is good and right and just and they cannot understand why you won't go along with it.

We all see ourselves as heroes. From the lowest level bureaucrat who justifies their actions right up to the dictator in chief. Every murderer and thief and gossip and wife beater and lazy worker in history has believed they were entitled to act as they did. They had to. We may be tempted to ourselves, because if we do something truly terrible, and are faced with the terrible thing we did, well we know what can happen:

> *"I have sinned," he said, "for I have betrayed innocent blood."*
> *"What is that to us?" they replied. "That's your responsibility."*
> *So Judas threw the money into the temple and left. Then he went away and hanged himself.*
> *Matthew 27:4-5*

That is how devastating our failure can be to us. Some people do take their own lives because they have done something and cannot live with the guilt and shame. I know that is only one reason people take their own lives, but it is a reason. We need people to understand that affirmation of a trans identity is harmful. We also need to give them a way to accept that without destroying them in the process. There is an extremely important statement in Paul's letter to the Roman church:

> *...for all have sinned*
> *and fall short of the glory of God...*
> *Romans 3:22-24*

I do believe that every Christian must come to a place of acknowledging their sin before God. If we can do this, if we can admit our failings, our mistakes, and oh so importantly, recognise that in God's eyes, it is all the same – my sin is no better than Hitler's. Stalin's sin is no worse than mine. The person who has hurt you or hurt me, their sin is no worse than yours or mine. It is so difficult for us to accept this – to level ourselves with every person who has ever done us wrong, who has ever hurt us and be able to look at them and say – I need God's forgiveness as much as they do. What they have done can be forgiven by God and by me. Just as God forgave me through Jesus, I can forgive and will forgive them.

Stella O'Malley once described the need to offer a golden bridge to those who affirmed gender identities, to provide a way for them to escape the trap they have created for themselves. An escape route. An off-ramp from the affirmation journey.

I think that only God can bring them to the place where they will realise they need this golden bridge. It is only his Holy Spirit that can convict them. Yet God may well want us to be the ones to greet them at the other side, or even call on them to cross over and help them do so. It may be the bravest, kindest, most generous thing you ever do to forgive a person – perhaps many people – who have affirmed your child in the trans lie. I know I am still struggling with this. God give us strength to forgive. And remember, Jesus commanded us to forgive and warned us what would happen if we do not:

And forgive us our debts,
as we also have forgiven our debtors.
And lead us not into temptation,
but deliver us from the evil one.'
For if you forgive other people when they sin against you, your heavenly Father will also forgive you. But if you do not forgive others their sins, your Father will not forgive your sins.
Matthew 6:12-15

Day 12: Heroes in their own story

I have struggled so much with this command of Jesus. How do I forgive people who continue to sin against me? Yet on the cross, that is exactly what Jesus did. And he expects me to follow his example. To be obedient to him. That is the heroic call made of every single follower of Christ – to forgive those who have wronged us.

Father in heaven, help me to examine myself with humility, to recognise and confess my sin. May I kneel before the cross of Jesus and see that it is my sin being paid for. And may I look at those who have hurt me, who have hurt my child, and understand that just as you forgave me, you also want to forgive them, and you want me to forgive them. Help me to forgive. Soften my hard heart that I can forgive. May I not make the mistake of Saul becoming arrogant and proudful, thinking myself better than others. Give me your love and compassion and mercy to be able to offer that golden bridge when the time is right. Amen

Day 13 — The belt of truth

> *Finally, be strong in the Lord and in his mighty power. Put on the full armour of God, so that you can take your stand against the devil's schemes. For our struggle is not against flesh and blood, but against the rulers, against the authorities, against the powers of this dark world and against the spiritual forces of evil in the heavenly realms. Therefore put on the full armour of God, so that when the day of evil comes, you may be able to stand your ground, and after you have done everything, to stand.*
> *Stand firm then, with the belt of truth buckled around your waist...*
> *Ephesians 6:10-14*

Why did Paul write this to the Ephesian church? Is it just a metaphor – the full armour of God? I certainly have not seen any Christian wandering round, laden down with heavy armour. It brings to mind the tale of the Emperor's New Clothes, only visible to the tailor (and yes, if you have not thought that trans reminds you of that tale, perhaps it would be worth re-reading it!) Yet the church in Paul's day and in the years that followed were in need of this counsel. I may not be able to pick up a belt of truth, but I have lived through a day of evil. Many of you reading this have experienced not just a day, but weeks, months, and even years of evil.

I've already written about being strong in the Lord, about the spiritual forces that our real battle is against, and perhaps I have not written enough, but in truth, I feel ignorant. So, acknowledging my ignorance, I would like to revisit this armour of God. Revisit because I've heard many preachers and teachers over the years encourage the church to use this spiritual armour. And it strikes me that truth is the first armour we need:

Stand firm then, with the belt of truth buckled around your waist…
Ephesians 6:14

Truth. I remember as a teenager arguing with atheists who rejected my claims that the bible was true. They said they only believed in facts. I did not have all the facts and so I often found myself uncertain how to respond. Somehow, facts have now been rejected by people who have had great influence in favour of a truth, a truth that can shift and change at a whim. I had a discussion with someone I love and they used the term: "My truth". I heard that and was immediately alert. If you have your truth and I have my truth, then truth is meaningless. I do not believe there is any real distinction between truth and fact. A fact is either true or it is not. A truth can be backed up by facts, or it can be true despite lack of evidence. We may not have facts yet, but something that is true does not need our limited knowledge to prove it.

We are commanded to accept gender identity as truth, as a fact. And my child may argue that I've just proved why I should accept their identity since their truth does not require facts. In response I find myself turning to the source of truth, Jesus:

Jesus answered, "I am the way and the truth and the life. No one comes to the Father except through me."
John 14:6

Day 13: The belt of truth

We face emotional blackmail, peer pressure, threats of exile, and being made an outcast. Against all this it is difficult to stand against the blackmail and all who try and manipulate us, demanding we submit to their view of the world, that we celebrate their perspective, encourage and support their beliefs. Who can help us defend against this onslaught? Jesus stands firm. Jesus was there at the beginning:

In the beginning was the Word, and the Word was with God, and the Word was God. He was with God in the beginning. Through him all things were made; without him nothing was made that has been made. In him was life, and that life was the light of all mankind. The light shines in the darkness, and the darkness has not overcome it.
John 1:1-5

Without Jesus, without the Word, without the Truth, nothing was made. Perhaps we could say that nothing could have been made? After all, how could the universe have been constructed if built on a lie, the shakiest of foundations? All things were made through the Truth — through Jesus, the Word. In Jesus was life and we also know this truth — that we were made male and female:

So God created mankind in his own image, in the image of God he created them; male and female he created them.
Genesis 1:27

The truth is that God created us. The truth is that we are created in the image of God. The truth is that we are created male and female. These truths stand firm against an assault on our sanity. Our child might want us to believe their truth, and there often is great pressure on us as parents to do just that. Yet a child's truth that is at odds with reality has potential for danger. If I was not already aware of trans ideology before I found out my child identified as trans, I don't know what I would have done. Would I have been tempted to go along with their identity, affirm them to maintain our relationship? It is possible. I don't know. I believe that my knowledge of what was happening in the wider world, and how I chose to respond to that – my expression of that knowledge – contributed to estrangement with my child and I know from painful experience that knowing the truth and speaking the truth does not prevent disaster. How we speak the truth matters. I failed in many ways, venting my anger and frustration in the hearing of my child. If I speak the truth but turn people away from me, how does that help them? Yet at the same time, others have reported that speaking gently and tiptoeing around the truth, has made little apparent difference to their children.

We are at war. Whether we like it or not, if our child has taken on a trans identity, war has come to our house, to our home. Truth is a weapon we can use, firstly to protect ourselves, to defend against the lies that trans seems to be built of. Questioning statements made is a powerful way to expose a lie and introduce truth. I've heard it said many times that we cannot force a person to believe. If we can help them to start questioning themselves and questioning what they have been told, then perhaps we allow truth to fight it's own battle in the mind of our child. Expressing our doubts and confusion is another method to introduce truth. I don't understand that, can you explain it to me? And none of us have to lie in doing that. The concept of a gender identity at odds with our physical body is confusing because there is no evidence for it. Instead if we meditate on the fact that God created us male and female we can quickly realise that each of us has been made male and female with aspects of our physical appearance, our personality, our interests, our character. And this then begs the question – if I as a man can have feminine characteristics and still be a man, and the reverse is true for all women, why does my child need drugs and surgeries when whatever masculine traits she has are already there?

We could explore the metaphor in greater and greater detail though this risks going beyond what was intended. A belt is used to hold up and to contain. If that belt is not buckled securely, not only will it fall off, everything attached to it will fall and clothes or additional armour will be unsecured leaving us vulnerable. Truth protects us, yes, and we must also secure what is true. Hold onto the truth. Hold onto the source of all truth – Jesus Christ.

Father in heaven, thank you for your son, the truth that sets us free, the truth that is our sure foundation, our rock that anchors us in this storm we find ourselves in. Fill us with your truth, help us to discern the truth and see where lies seek to undermine us. Give us your wisdom and guide us in how we should speak with our child and with others, to share the truth, to question anything that we are concerned about, to express our doubts and confusion in a way that exposes lies and allows your truth to shine. Amen

Day 14 — The breastplate of righteousness

Stand firm then, with the belt of truth buckled around your waist, with the breastplate of righteousness in place...
Ephesians 6:14

I have struggled to write this chapter. I felt it was important to try and apply the great teaching on the armour of God to our situation. And then I came undone as I looked into Righteousness. Paul tells us in Ephesians 6 to stand firm with the breastplate of righteousness in place. I had to ask myself – what does righteousness mean? It likely is a familiar word if you have grown up in the church or are familiar with Christian teaching. Yet I felt I had a mental block when I tried to grasp how I should interpret the term. Righteousness. What is righteousness?

I did a deep dive into righteousness, looking up all the passages where the term is used. As I did, I became more and more convicted. If you start in Genesis – and Genesis is always a good place to start – we find believing God is the first recorded definition of righteousness:

He took him outside and said, "Look up at the sky and count the stars—if indeed you can count them." Then he said to him, "So shall your offspring be." Abram believed the Lord, and he credited it to him as righteousness.
Genesis 15:5-6

Then the term righteousness is not mentioned until

Moses uses it to describe those who obey God:

> **The Lord commanded us to obey all these decrees and to fear the Lord our God, so that we might always prosper and be kept alive, as is the case today. And if we are careful to obey all this law before the Lord our God, as he has commanded us, that will be our righteousness."**
> **Deuteronomy 6:24-25**

So, we have two definitions which I feel are very closely related: You are righteous if you believe God and if you obey him. And why wouldn't you obey God if you believe in him. The opposite is self-evidently true – if I don't believe someone I am not likely to obey them.

Then the definition broadens. In Psalm 106 we find righteousness credited to Phinehas and have to flip back to Numbers 25 to find out what Phinehas did. The Israelites as a nation were being punished for their collective behaviour – sexual immorality as part of idol worship – punished with a plague that took the lives of 24,000. The Israelites recognised their sinful activity had been the cause of their punishment and they repented, only not all of them. We are told that while the whole nation was weeping in repentance before the Lord, one Israelite, Zimri son of Salu, defiantly proceeded to walk past them with one of the women that had tempted the men and took her into his tent to have sex with her. Phinehas executed them both and this is God's response:

> **The Lord said to Moses, "Phinehas son of Eleazar, the son of Aaron, the priest, has turned my anger away from the Israelites. Since he was as zealous for my honor among them as I am, I did not put an end**

Day 14: The breastplate of righteousness

to them in my zeal. Therefore tell him I am making my covenant of peace with him. He and his descendants will have a covenant of a lasting priesthood, because he was zealous for the honor of his God and made atonement for the Israelites."
Numbers 25:10-13

Righteousness now expands to include being zealous for God's honour. And the definition expands still further when we get to Proverbs:

The integrity of the upright guides them, but the unfaithful are destroyed by their duplicity.
Wealth is worthless in the day of wrath, but righteousness delivers from death.
The righteousness of the blameless makes their paths straight, but the wicked are brought down by their own wickedness.
Proverbs 11:3-5

Righteousness here is associated with integrity, with being upright, being without blame, and also walking a straight path. These descriptions are contrasted with what must be the opposite of righteousness: being unfaithful, being duplicitous, being wicked. And I read through all these descriptions and definitions and my heart sinks as I cannot say I have lived a life that has been consistent, that has lived up to the highest standards righteousness seems to demand. But I keep reading and eventually get to Romans, a letter I find difficult to understand, complicated, full of deep thoughts, and I am taken right back to the very first definition in Genesis:

What does Scripture say? "Abraham believed God, and it was credited to him as righteousness."
Romans 4:3

And Paul goes on to encourage us even more:

"Blessed are those whose transgressions are forgiven, whose sins are covered.
Blessed is the one whose sin the Lord will never count against them."
Romans 4:7-8

Can it be? Can you and I experience this blessing, of our sin and transgression being forgiven and covered over and never counted against us?

Nor can the gift of God be compared with the result of one man's sin: The judgement followed one sin and brought condemnation, but the gift followed many trespasses and brought justification. For if, by the trespass of the one man, death reigned through that one man, how much more will those who receive God's abundant provision of grace and of the gift of righteousness reign in life through the one man, Jesus Christ!
Consequently, just as one trespass resulted in condemnation for all people, so also one righteous act resulted in justification and life for all people.
Romans 5:16-18

Yes! It is not our own righteousness that we take as a breastplate to protect us, but the righteousness of Jesus Christ who was without sin, who lived an upright life, who led a straight path, who believed God his Father, and was obedient to him, who was zealous for his Father. Finally, ultimately, Jesus humbled himself through obedience to his Father, to allow himself to become a sacrifice for us – the scapegoat effectively – as described in Leviticus 16.

I must humble myself to recognise my own lack of righteousness, and in taking on the breastplate of Jesus' righteousness, I do not continue in my own unrighteousness, instead I allow Jesus to transform my life, my heart, my desires so that I want to believe God, I want to obey God, I want to live a life that is zealous and upright and following the path that Jesus walked.

And I realise now that in all this study and thought, I've not once mentioned trans! Or have I? I look back over what I've quoted and written and find these statements: 'Blessed are those whose transgressions are forgiven', and 'I allow Jesus to transform my life'.

I have been trying to think of a title for this book. Normally I get the title first and the book is strongly influenced by that title, but in this case I only had a working title: Transformed. Recently I wondered about using From Transgression to Transformed. Trans is a strange term. Perhaps our children use it as an abbreviation for transformed or transition. It is rarely clear what they mean since we humans can do neither. We cannot transform from male to female and cannot transition from woman to man, or vice versa. And when our children start talking about gender, what they appear to be doing is confusing our cultural expectations of masculine and feminine with biology.

I believe that trans is a transgression. Firstly, anyone who chooses to believe they are trans is transgressing against themselves. The elevation of a lie over truth, of a fiction in preference over reality. This transgression of thought and belief leads so very often to experimental drugs and dangerous surgery. Then trans is a transgression against those around us, attempting to co-opt us into believing the lie, gaslighting us and punishing us when we resist. Ultimately it is a transgression against our creator, saying I don't need you, I reject your image, I'm going to remake myself in my image.

But if our righteousness is in Jesus, then we start from a very different perspective. Jesus is the truth and so he can lead us to acceptance of our body. Jesus is a healer and it may be for some that whether the healing we need is emotional, mental, or physical, that Jesus can and will answer our request for healing. I'm reminded of the account of Jesus and a man born blind in John 9.

> *As he went along, he saw a man blind from birth. His disciples asked him, "Rabbi, who sinned, this man or his parents, that he was born blind?"*
>
> *"Neither this man nor his parents sinned," said Jesus, "but this happened so that the works of God might be displayed in him. As long as it is day, we must do the works of him who sent me. Night is coming, when no one can work. While I am in the world, I am the light of the world."*
>
> *After saying this, he spit on the ground, made some mud with the saliva, and put it on the man's eyes. "Go," he told him, "wash in the Pool of Siloam" (this word means "Sent"). So the man went and washed, and came home seeing.*
>
> *John 9:1-7*

For some of our children, not all but some, it is possible that the gender dysphoria they suffer from has been allowed that Jesus will one day heal them of it, allowing them to experience the healing of God. You might say –

wouldn't it be better if they never suffered in the first place? Yet, don't we all suffer? Who am I and who are you to say that experience might not in the end be incredibly precious and valuable?

There is so much more that could be said but I feel I need to limit myself and stay on track. In this war, in our daily battles even with our trans identified child, we need the protection that Jesus' righteousness offers us. To know our sins have been forgiven, that God loves and accepts us. The hate we can experience from our child and other loved ones threatens to destroy us. The breastplate of righteousness protects our heart, and allows us to know the love of God.

Father in heaven, thank you for your love, displayed in your son Jesus Christ. Thank you for your gift of righteousness for those of us who believe in Jesus, those of us who have accepted your son's sacrifice for our sin. Lead us Father to believe you, to believe what you have told us and continue to tell us. May we obey your commands and honour you in all our lives. Guide us to live lives of integrity and to seek to walk your narrow path. Protect us, protect our hearts from the attacks of the enemy. Protect us from the attacks of our child. Protect our children from those who seek to steal our children away from us and from you. And deliver our children from the beliefs that have stolen their hearts. Fill them with your love and break the hold that trans has over them. Amen

Day 15 — The gospel of peace

...and with your feet fitted with the readiness that comes from the gospel of peace.
Ephesians 6:15

If you search on the word peace found in the combined books of the Bible, you will find it used well over 200 times. Jesus alone blesses many after he has healed or delivered them telling them again and again: "Go in peace." What is the "gospel of peace"? Is it not peace with God. Jesus' priority was to forgive people their sins. The healings, the resurrections from the dead, these all took second place to Jesus' main ambition, to save as many as he could from eternal death, reconciling them to his Father in heaven, to our God. And yet at the same time, Jesus made it clear that peace with God does not mean peace on earth, not even in our home:

"I have come to bring fire on the earth, and how I wish it were already kindled! But I have a baptism to undergo, and what constraint I am under until it is completed! Do you think I came to bring peace on earth? No, I tell you, but division. From now on there will be five in one family divided against each other, three against two and two against three. They will be divided, father against son and son against father, mother against daughter and daughter against mother, mother-in-law against daughter-in-law and daughter-in-law against mother-in-law."
Luke 12:49-53

For those living with a trans identified child in your home, this warning of Jesus may be one you are living with on a minute by minute basis. For myself, even estranged from my children and in conflict with many members of my family, I see this scenario played out. My children and some others in my family may claim that they are the ones following Jesus' instruction, interpreting his command to love as guiding them to affirm my child. And so, we are not at peace, me and my children, me and so many in my family. I can understand what might drive some to affirm in order to be at peace, to attempt to rescue the relationship. The cost seems too high to me. It cannot be peace if one party is held hostage by another. And since Jesus stated he did not come to bring us peace with our family, why should that be our top priority?

If as I understand it, Paul was encouraging us to be ready to share a gospel of reconciliation with God, that is quite different from encouraging us to affirm a child's desires. Or even to attempt to save a child from their obvious distress in believing they are in the wrong body. Peace as Paul is referring to – reconciliation with God – often results in conflict with those close to us on earth. Anyone in fact who attempts to change their life will often experience opposition and conflict. It seems we humans are deeply suspicious of change – even and sometimes especially change for the better. Seeing someone else improve their life can cause us to feel guilty that we are not doing more. It can trigger feelings of jealousy and resentment. We can be dismissive – they think they are better than us. And this is a contradiction since often the person trying to change, the person choosing reconciliation with God has recognised they are no better than anyone else, in fact, conviction of sin may lead us to think we are the worst of all people. But if someone watching us is not willing to examine themselves that closely, is not yet willing to humble themselves, my choice or your choice to recognise our weakness and failings and sin can be a great obstacle to the one who is not yet ready. And I believe this is why Jesus gave us his warning about division in the family.

What application can this have for our child? A child who may be angered by our attempts to "preach" at them, to challenge them, to question them? Truly we need the wisdom of God. Each situation may require a different response or may require us to act or speak in a unique way. Jesus showed us that it is possible to act as an individual needs us to – he is recorded as using as many different approaches as the people he met. We need the daily and sometimes minute by minute guidance of the Holy Spirit. This in itself requires each of us to humble ourselves – not to assume we know what must be said or done, and to live a life of trust and faith. Sometimes taking great risks, in the hope that either God is guiding us, or that God will work all things together for good for those who love him and are called according to his purpose.

I want my child to find peace in their body, to be able to accept themselves without having to take radical steps to change their appearance. Yet God's priority is reconciliation with my child. Just as Jesus frequently chose to forgive sins and healing seemed like more of an afterthought, so from God's perspective, my child being reconciled with him is most important. It is possible that my desire and God's may be in conflict. And even though it tears at me, God must overcome – even my desire.

If we follow Christ, we are expected to be ready to help reconcile others with God. And thinking about this strange metaphor of armour that Paul is using, this battle that we are in, for the very souls of our children, we are seeking both to reconcile and be reconciled ourselves. As we are ourselves reconciled with God, our step is lighter, our burdens cast off. The road may be narrow, but the way is straight. God desires to be reconciled with our children. God may use us to bring about that reconciliation if we will listen to him, submit to him and humble ourselves. It is a gospel of peace with God. But to get there we may have to endure conflict and strife and division. So buckle up your spiritual sandals, there may be a rocky path ahead!

Father in heaven, thank you that you first forgave us, you sought reconciliation with us, you desired peace with us. Bless you and praise you that you have offered us and have given us your forgiveness and your peace. May we bless our children and even those who have worked against us that they too might be reconciled with you. That they too can be forgiven and find your peace. Have mercy on our children, Father, as you had mercy on us. Show us how to share your gospel of peace with our child. And if the time is not right, if we must give our children space and time so that they can mature and come to an understanding themselves of risk and danger and consequences, then please, guide our children through this valley of the shadow of death and bring them out into your light. Deliver them where they can be delivered, and where their will is too stubborn and their heart too hard, where they have been so deceived that they cannot think straight, have mercy on them and call them to know your peace. Do not give up on them and strengthen us that we will continue to seek their reconciliation with you. Amen

Day 16 — The shield of faith

In addition to all this, take up the shield of faith, with which you can extinguish all the flaming arrows of the evil one.
Ephesians 6:16

When Satan cannot overtly destroy you, he will attempt to seduce you, corrupt you, or undermine your faith in God. In my reading through the book of Numbers I've reached the account of Balaam being asked to curse Israel. The Moabites were terrified at the sight of the Israelites camped along the Jordan river. They feared that Israel would stay on the East side of the river and invade the territory of Moab. Fearing this, they called on Balaam to curse Israel. The account in Numbers chapters 22 to 25 first has Balaam refusing the call to curse. Then reluctantly travelling to Moab. Then he blesses Israel three times despite the anger of the king of Moab. Then finally, as is revealed later in chapter 31, we have Balaam suggesting that the women of Moab seduce the men of Israel, leading them to bow down before idols.

The evil one is restrained in what he can do to those who love the Lord, to those who are called by God. The same pattern is repeated again and again. Our loving Father in heaven will allow us to suffer. To suffer as Job did. But even then, the evil one could not destroy Job, only punish him in the hope he might turn against his creator. We see in the book of Nehemiah that the enemies of Israel attempted to undermine Nehemiah's work at rebuilding the defences of Jerusalem. They spread rumours about him and would have drawn him out of safety to a place where they could have killed him, but Nehemiah recognised their devious intent and stayed true to his calling.

We find that Satan attempted to murder God's only son through Herod, leading the ruler over Israel to slaughter the infants. Through visions and dreams, the protectors of the infant Jesus were led to safety. And when Jesus returned as an adult to begin the work God had commanded him to do, Satan revealed his true nature, once again using seduction. This time Satan used promises of power and wealth – to tempt Jesus to turn from his Father in heaven.

Satan would destroy us as well. He may well succeed if we let him. Satan wants to destroy our families and this keeps me awake at night as the children of Job were killed by the evil one. Many infants were killed at the order of Herod, just as centuries before Israel's children were killed at the order of Pharaoh. Yet Moses was spared as Jesus was and some of our children will be spared because God has a plan for them that neither we nor they yet know of. Yet not all of our children will be spared. Not all have been.

We are not promised a life free from pain. We are not promised that our children will be protected from all harm. Jesus warned us that terrible things would happen and warned those who would lead our children astray:

"If anyone causes one of these little ones—those who believe in me—to stumble, it would be better for them to have a large millstone hung around their neck and to be drowned in the depths of the sea. Woe to the world because of the things that cause people to stumble! Such things must come, but woe to the person through whom they come! If your hand or your

foot causes you to stumble, cut it off and throw it away. It is better for you to enter life maimed or crippled than to have two hands or two feet and be thrown into eternal fire.
Matthew 18:6-8

We cannot control our children. If they choose to follow the evil one, all we can do is warn them. And if they do not listen to us, all we have left is to seek God for their protection, and we must raise the shield of faith, even over children who have turned away, trusting that our Father in Heaven will have mercy on them.

And some of our children are led astray, not because of any evil intent in their heart, but because they have been deceived. We must raise the shield of faith over them, asking God to open their eyes to the lies and the deceit and to lead them into the truth. And we know that Jesus is the way and the truth and the life. I referred to these words of Jesus in another chapter:

However, when the Son of Man comes, will he find faith on the earth?"
Luke 18:8

Satan wants to destroy us so much that he will use our children if he can. And how devastating it is for those who have lost their children or have seen their children do terrible things to themselves that cannot be undone! It is almost a crippling blow – a canon ball rather than an arrow, one that risks shattering whatever shield of faith we may attempt to put up. There are many terrible and evil things that can test our faith in God to the limit. Paul is using a metaphor here. An important and valuable one. Yet it is only a metaphor. If you doubt God, this does not mean you cannot again choose to have faith in him. If you abandon hope in God, this does not mean you cannot repent and turn back to him in faith he will receive you. The shield of faith is not a literal shield that can be shattered and never used again.

I wonder if a different metaphor may be useful to help us understand Paul's metaphor of the shield of faith – the force field – as found in many science fictions movies and TV series. These fictional shields can be weakened by repeated attacks. They require energy to sustain them. If an essential component fails, they switch off entirely leaving one completely helpless. Our faith can be weakened by repeated attacks. God knows this and we see Jesus withdrawing to a quiet place again and again, to pray and be close to his father. If the son of God needed to retreat from attacks, how much more do we need to do this? And Jesus in a most revealing statement once asked who had touched him stating that power had gone out of him. His energy level was reduced – by the faith of the woman who had suffered from bleeding. Jesus' power healed the woman, at a cost to himself. And what does it take for someone to be left completely vulnerable to attack from the evil one? I've been thinking about Judas a lot recently. Judas betrayed Jesus. This morning I read this:

> **"Cursed is anyone who accepts a bribe to kill an innocent person."**
> **Deuteronomy 27:25**

Judas is described as cursed. The one destined to be cursed. Why? He accepted a bribe to kill the only innocent man ever to have lived a full life on this Earth. Having done this evil and despicable thing, Judas had effectively switched off his shield of faith. Completely disconnected it

Day 16: The shield of faith

and was vulnerable to the devil's leading him to take his own life. As I've thought about Judas I've wondered, could Judas have been forgiven? Perhaps you might think me naive for asking this, yet it troubles me. What was Judas' sin? I feel it was a betrayal. And so many people I love have – I believe – betrayed me. Can I forgive them? I feel I must. And so – would Jesus have been able to forgive Judas? I feel he would. I look at Peter's betrayal of Jesus and Jesus took time to gently lead Peter back into relationship and reconciliation. I know I am speculating. It seems clear to me that Jesus knew beforehand that Judas would betray him and as far as we know, Jesus made no attempt to persuade Judas not to do so. Yet I can also see so many warnings littered throughout Jesus' teaching that Judas must have heard. And so ultimately I believe that Judas let down his guard, turned off the faith that might have spared him from the attack of the evil one, and so was defenceless against the final attack.

Over two years ago I thought about ending my life. Thanks be to God I recognised this as an evil thought. I believe God spoke to me, even if only through the tumult of thoughts in my head, and helped me to see that if I ended my life, that would be a victory for evil. So much evil has been done. Some of our children have suffered so much because of the evil that is trans. Would it not be better to say enough! Evil may have been done to my child. Evil may yet take my child, yet I will choose to raise the shield of faith in God and in his son Jesus and will not let the devil have one more victory.

Father in heaven, thank you that you do not leave us defenceless. Thank you that you give us faith, and that faith is in you and you are trustworthy. Bless you that you warned us in advance that we would suffer.

Thank you that you gave us your wisdom and the accounts of so many who suffered before us, who were able to continue in their faith in you. Strengthen us, Father. Strengthen our faith in you. Where we are weak, help us to take time to rest in you and be recharged in our faith. Where we are under constant attack, show us how and where we can retreat to allow us to re-centre ourselves in you. And if we ever go too far, ever make a mistake that seems like it cannot be undone, remind us that you still love us and want to forgive us and reconcile with us. Amen

Day 17 — The helmet of salvation

Take the helmet of salvation...
Ephesians 6:17

Why are we looking at the armour of God? What relevance does it have to those of us with children who identify as trans? Well, I believe we are at war. And the person in a war-zone who does not wear a helmet is asking to get shot in the head. Too blunt? Perhaps. Helmets are no guarantee of safety. My wife enjoys visiting castles and old buildings and while I don't enjoy that experience as much, I am fascinated by how those old buildings are constructed and what they often contain. Walk round many castles and you will often find suits of armour, and a variety of different types of helmet.

We recently went to Alnwick Castle and briefly joined a group learning about different types of helmet. A couple of helmets stood out to me: one which looked very much like a bucket, sloping sides, but with a flat top; and the one that replaced it – curving up to a point. In Paul's time, the two greatest risks a soldier faced likely were swords and arrows. In a face to face fight with your enemy, that bucket shaped helmet might have stopped a sword from cutting your head in two, but it would have rang like a bell if the sword came swinging down on that flat top. You may well have been concussed and if the metal was not strong enough, it probably would have buckled, leaving you knocked out and unable to defend yourself against a killing blow. The curved helmet on the other hand may just have saved your life, deflecting that downward stroke. Of course, you would then need armour on your shoulders to stop a different kind of serious injury, yet at least your head would be spared.

Take the helmet of salvation, Paul encourages us. A helmet protects us where we are most vulnerable. I'm reminded of the old movie: Highlander – if your head comes away from your body, it is all over.

Salvation – it is our greatest protection. Without the death and resurrection of Jesus, we would be left with the old covenant of sacrifice. A set of laws that no-one could live up to. And Jesus fulfilled all of that old law through his sacrifice for us. We were saved, through Jesus, through his death on the cross, through the blood he shed. Jesus became a curse for us, in our place, that we could receive the blessing of God.

I've heard so many stories from people whose children identify as trans. It unmoors us, threatens to destabilise us to such an extent that life itself may not seem worth living. Betrayals, deceptions, lies built upon lies. Each of us needs something solid to stand on when our world is threatened to this extent. The salvation offered through Jesus Christ is a defence we can rely on. All our sin, all our weakness, all our failures paid for on the cross. I have beat myself up over and over about all the ways I failed as a father. Yet Jesus paid for my sin. My child may not yet be able to forgive me for whatever they think I have done, but Jesus already has forgiven me for all wrong I have done. My child may disown me, but Jesus offers out his hand to me, just as he effectively did to the murderer hanging next to him on that cross. Members of my family, some of my friends, colleagues, and neighbours may have chosen to affirm my child, yet Jesus affirms the truth. He is the way and the truth and the life. He is our salvation.

Salvation is not a word I think of as being in common

Day 17: The helmet of salvation

use today. Perhaps it is used and is known about, after all, hostages are saved, as are kidnap victims. Some people are saved from would be rapists or murderers. And I suspect all of us know what salvation is because so many are not saved and we wish they had been.

For a while now I've been struggling with thoughts connected to salvation. I have it in mind to write a short prayer / study guide looking at the Good News, or as Christians refer to it – the Gospel of Jesus Christ. Good News is a better term than Gospel, I feel. Yet it is a very strange sort of good news. And Salvation is very much part of that strange good news. Salvation: To be saved. But from what? Well, sin and death. Except, those who choose to follow Jesus still sin and all of us die. So... what is it we are being saved from? Well, really, it is the eternal consequences of sin and death. Sin being all of the bad choices we make, all the actions and words that cause pain and hurt and suffering to others. Death being the second death, the one that many, even those who call themselves Christian refuse to believe in. We will all die, that we can all agree on. It is what happens after death that we need salvation for – the final judgement:

Then I saw a great white throne and him who was seated on it. The earth and the heavens fled from his presence, and there was no place for them. And I saw the dead, great and small, standing before the throne, and books were opened. Another book was opened, which is the book of life. The dead were judged according to what they had done as recorded in the books. The sea gave up the dead that were in it, and death and Hades gave up the dead that were in them, and each person was judged according to what they had done. Then death and Hades were thrown into

> ***the lake of fire. The lake of fire is the second death. Anyone whose name was not found written in the book of life was thrown into the lake of fire.***
> ***Revelation 20:11-15***

When I wrote my first 31 Days of Prayer book, I shared it with my parents and my father challenged me on my ambivalence over the existence of an eternal Hell. Jesus refers to Hell in different ways in different teaching. Why would he do that if Hell does not or will not exist. Even in my ambivalence that made no sense to me. I do not believe Jesus said a single thing that was without value. If Jesus thought it was important enough to warn of the dangers of a judgement after we die, I believe we should take his warning seriously. Jesus took the possibility of Hell so seriously that he willingly submitted his life to torture and death on a cross so that we could have salvation. And for anyone still tempted to argue back – if there is no Hell, why did Jesus determine it so necessary to die on the cross?

For those of us struggling with our children having rejected their birth sex, some of us will also have watched in horror as along with that stable foundation they have also rejected the salvation offered through Jesus. I have heard many parents who do not believe in God write about the hell they are going through. The hell they are watching their children embrace. Hell is horrific. The horrors we witness suggest to me that there is an ultimate horror, a Hell which every person is at risk of being thrown into at the final judgement.

I remember clearly that several times during my childhood, I was so convicted that I was going to Hell that I sought Jesus' salvation. Eventually, aged 19, I received what is called the filling of the Holy Spirit, a physical

Day 17: The helmet of salvation

experience of God, and for the first time in my young life had assurance of salvation.

I have had times of doubt since, uncertainty whether being once saved means I am always saved. Yet it is good for me to remember that the helmet of salvation is a metaphor, and that we do not take our salvation, instead we receive salvation. It is given by God through his son Jesus. If I doubt, if you doubt, whether we are saved, we can always go back to the one who saves us and ask him to confirm again that our salvation is secure. If you do not know the salvation that Jesus offers you, I encourage you to seek his salvation today. I know that salvation may not spare us from the horror we face today or tomorrow, yet it will spare us from the ultimate horror of being rejected by God for all eternity and in that I can take some comfort. I pray for my child to find salvation in Jesus, to be spared the horror of gender affirming surgery. But if my child persists down this road to pain and suffering, I will continue to pray for them that God will lead them to salvation in Jesus. In the end we are told that those who receive the salvation of Jesus have this promise waiting for them:

'He will wipe every tear from their eyes. There will be no more death' or mourning or crying or pain, for the old order of things has passed away."
Revelation 21:4

There is hope for those who find salvation in Jesus. Even after irreversible treatments and surgeries. Hope that might allow some to continue living and overcome the tragedies they were deceived into. One day, there will be healing, even from the horror of what has been done through trans.

Father in heaven, thank you for the gift of salvation through Jesus your son. I believe that Jesus died for me, for my child, and for all who will accept the gift of salvation you offer. Father, please help me to trust in your salvation, to look forward to the promise of healing, especially when facing the darkest horrors. Protect me and my family. Deliver my child from this horror. Lead them out of the deception, save them even from themselves. Amen

Day 18

The sword of the Spirit

...and the sword of the Spirit,
which is the word of God.
Ephesians 6:17

How we treat the word of God is a most peculiar thing. Some who claim to be followers of Christ will disparage it, claim that it is a fiction, that much of it is simply poetry and a set of myths. Others go to a different extreme, unable to see the nuance in some commands assuming they are for all time and all situations when even Jesus would say one thing at one time, and then command something different when the context had changed.

In my youth, I came to feel that I had made my copy of the Bible an idol. I loved the teaching and the stories and believed God spoke to me through what I read, yet the very book had become so important to me that once when some colleagues played a joke on me and hid it, I became distraught. After I got the book back I tried to learn that the physical copy of the Bible was not something to obsess over.

I have found that there is tremendous power in the word of God, that the Spirit of the Lord can speak to me and others through it. I have found so much comfort in reading the word of God. I have been guided by it, rebuked by it, I have found that my perception of the world around me has been aided, clarified, and corrected.

The Holy Bible is a set of books, some of which are historical accounts and I believe they are as reliable as any others, more so than most. The fact that the heroes of the stories are frequently condemned for their actions, the most evil things they do laid bare gives me confidence these are not books of lies, but rather humble confessions of what actually happened. If the historical books were made up as some claim, why would those in authority to decide what would be included have presented themselves in such a bad light?

There is poetry in the books of the bible, and fiction. It is not always clear which is fiction and which is historical account. The book of Job in particular stands out as I consider them now. I have heard a preacher claim that it must be fiction because it was grouped together with the books of poetry: the Psalms and Proverbs. I do not know. It is similar with the account of the creation. Mankind did not witness either the formation of the solar system or the meeting of Satan and God to decide Job's fate. But there would have been a trustworthy witness: God himself. And if God met with Moses and told him what to write as a record of creation, then why couldn't the same thing have happened to the author who wrote down the account of Job? I do not know. I do know however that whether fact as we might understand it today, or poetry, there are deep truths found in both the account of creation and Job.

I realised early on after being told my child identified as trans that I was living out a tragedy similar to that of Job. Within a few hours, almost all that I held dear was ripped away from me, it felt like all that was left was for the earth to open up and swallow me down into Hell. I identified so closely with how Job must have felt as he sat on the ashes, scraping himself with broken pottery. Curse God and die, his wife suggested. And some of you reading this may have or had a partner who suggested or even demanded worse of you. Demanded you affirm your child's belief, ignore your concerns, your doubts, your fears and embrace

Day 18: The sword of the Spirit

something that is evil. When those closest to you encourage you to sin, who has strength to resist? I was fortunate that my wife never encouraged me to affirm my child. But she was under so much pressure herself. I feared she would be seduced, that her love for her children would lead her to affirm before my wife knew of the long-term risks.

We are all susceptible to being influenced by those around us. It can be very difficult to resist social pressure. I had a lifetime of hearing the parables of Jesus where he talked about the foolish man being swept away by the flood – a picture of the massed and crushing pressure from government and the media and colleagues, friends and family who insist that all who identify as trans must be affirmed – while the wise man stayed firm on the rock, a symbol and picture of Jesus. A lifetime of hearing again and again the account of Noah, the sinful world swept away by the flood, the few who listened to God saved in an ark. Our home became an ark, where we desperately prayed to God for salvation – for us and for our children. You don't have to read far through the books of the bible before you find someone facing a trial. A test of their faith in God, of their commitment to truth or justice or mercy.

Everything that happened to us, everything that was said to us, I processed it through the filter of the word of God. Does this fit? Does it make sense knowing what Jesus said, or the Apostles taught? How does it mesh with the accounts of the prophets or the Kings of Israel or the experience of Moses or the Judges of Israel? If you read these books, you will find ordinary men and women and even children who face sometimes ordinary problems and sometimes extraordinary ones. You will find those that act well and those that fail miserably. You will read of the consequences of both, and in truth, you will find that those who face the most difficult trials will sometimes suffer and die in their suffering. Yet that will not be the end. We are not promised that our children will be spared the consequences of their actions. They may need to live with those consequences. Yet even if they choose unwisely, even if they reject God now, there is still hope that they can repent and be saved. Our God pursues us to rescue us and he pursues our children to rescue them if they will allow themselves to be rescued.

I love the word of God. I feel the word of God exposes my weaknesses and failings and allows me to view others with a better perspective, seeing I am no better than they, and God loves them as much as he loves me. The more you read it, the more you ask God to help you understand it, the better prepared you will be to defend yourself against lies and deceit and those who would lead you down a dark path. The better prepared to pray and seek God's mercy for our children and others.

Father in heaven, thank you for your word, the books you have caused to be written throughout the long years, the accounts of your servants and those who despised you, those who followed you and those who disobeyed. Thank you for showing the consequences both of obedience and disobedience. Help me to read your word with an open mind and be waiting for the leading of your Holy Spirit. To be wise and to receive your wisdom even as I read. Guide me through your word, lead me and help me to find the hope you offer. Amen

Day 19 — Pray in the Spirit

Take the helmet of salvation and the sword of the Spirit, which is the word of God.
And pray in the Spirit on all occasions with all kinds of prayers and requests. With this in mind, be alert and always keep on praying for all the Lord's people.
Ephesians 6:17-18

I felt that I had to separate the above statements, to explore them individually, and yet when I was writing yesterday's chapter, I had a sense that they are also to be combined – that the helmet of salvation and sword of the spirit are necessary preconditions to enable us to pray in the spirit. If we are not saved through the blood of Jesus, if we have never believed in Jesus' death and resurrection and his sacrifice for our sin, how can we have confidence that God will hear and answer us? If we do not know the word of God, if we can not remind God of his promises, plead with him on the basis of what he has revealed through his word, we are effectively disarmed. It is not that God will not hear you if you do not know God's word very well, or that he will not listen to the cry of someone who has not yet believed, and so if this describes you, then do pray to God, do seek him for it may be that your desire to save your child, to be rescued from this situation will lead you to salvation and lead you to read God's word for yourself and so you will find yourself transformed.

I am susceptible to periods of depression. I've managed to avoid a clinical diagnosis yet I alternate between mood swings that lead me to believe I can conquer the world and conviction that I am the world's worst sinner and believing that God cannot bear to listen to me. The helmet of salvation is a metaphor, of course. It describes a fact – that those of us who did respond to Jesus' call to repent, who chose to believe in his death and sacrifice in payment for our sin will in the end be saved from the second death. Jesus' return to life demonstrates that all of us will also be brought back to life. Each will face the ultimate judgement, and those of us who believed in Jesus will be saved, those who have not will be cast out. The metaphor also describes a choice we can make – to trust in this salvation and hope for our future in the face of danger and threat. There is no greater danger, no worse threat than to lose one's salvation. But as a friend of mine frequently says – no-one can take your salvation away from you. It may though be possible we can give it away. Why would we do that? How would we do that? Jesus warned his followers to stay on the straight path, to obey his commands. Even if we do this, Jesus warned that we would suffer if we follow him. He shared the parable of the sower indicating that some who seem to have fully embraced their salvation will turn away. Let us not be found among their number. If we hold fast to Jesus, if we continue to seek him, his salvation will rest on us and we can have confidence he is interceding for us before the throne of God:

...but because Jesus lives forever, he has a permanent priesthood. Therefore he is able to save completely those who come to God through him, because he always lives to intercede for them. Such a high priest truly meets our need—one who is holy, blameless, pure, set apart from sinners, exalted above the heavens.
Hebrews 7:24-26

If we are assured of our salvation and if we choose to read through the books of the bible, to study the teaching of Jesus and see how his life and death fulfils the prophecies made hundreds and thousands of years before, how his sacrifice fulfils the laws of sacrifice given to the Israelites through Moses, if we read the promises of God, and can begin to understand God's tactics and strategies, then we have a powerful weapon of defence and of attack to use in prayer. Prayer for our child, for our family, for the society around us.

There will be many occasions to pray for our child, many situations that it would benefit us and them to give up to God. I have to be honest with you, I struggle to give up my child to God. It is not that I don't trust God, it is that I feel I will always have the responsibility of being a parent. I think that's a good thing. I doubt that God wants us to stop praying for our children. So maybe I can put it like this. I need to keep reminding myself that I cannot control this situation, and that God sees the full picture, and God knows who and what is really influencing my child. Remember how Paul introduces the need for the armour of God:

For our struggle is not against flesh and blood, but against the rulers, against the authorities, against the powers of this dark world and against the spiritual forces of evil in the heavenly realms.
Ephesians 6:12

What does that even mean! I suspect that even many atheists, confronted with the hold that trans has over their child, will be aware of something unseen and sinister that appears to be a lot like a demonic influence. This warning of Paul's stands out because there is so little else in God's word about "the spiritual forces of evil". Possibly because as we are warned elsewhere, we are not to seek after such forces, not to have anything to do with them. Probably because we do not need to have anything to do with them to stand against them. When Jesus encountered a demon, he commanded it to leave the person that was suffering. Is it possible my child, or any of our children have some demonic influence over them? I don't know. I do not want to make any claims I cannot substantiate. Yet I do believe there is something inherently evil operating in or through those who promote and advocate for trans. I see this in the callous way that any risks to people are ignored or minimised. I see this in the so called "treatments" that leave so many suffering. I see it in the promises made which in the end are exposed like fool's gold. I see it in the claims that if you do this, your suffering will be eased, and yet so many continue to suffer.

    I feel helpless, powerless, confused, and uncertain. And so I pray. I pray for my child, and for the children of people who once were strangers. I pray that my government will finally begin to govern well and put an end to this madness. I pray for those I work for and with that their eyes will be opened to the damage that has been done. I pray that children and young people will be rescued out of what appears to me to be a cult.

    I have been fortunate to find a group of men to pray with, fathers like myself who have trans identified children. We pray for each other and for our children. Ultimately, I believe it is only God who can rescue them, who can break through whatever hold trans has over them. Not that I stop attempting to show my child I love her, but even then, I feel it will take a miracle for her to respond to those expressions of love. Friends have joined with us regularly to pray for our child. Their support has helped us survive what has been a brutal time.

Paul tells us to pray in the Spirit. So many times my wife and I have joined with others to pray, not having a clue what will make a difference. We have had to ask God to help us know what to pray for. And usually, he tells us. Somehow, stumbling, we seem to be given something to pray for and as we pray, a certainty grows – faith – that the prayer is not only to God, but is from God. That we are praying in the Spirit. It is as we admit our weakness and need for God that he lifts us up and shows us what to ask for.

Poor me. Look at how in need I am. It isn't a good look, is it! Sometimes though, we have to ask others for help. We have to admit our need. Then, those who truly care about us can show their love for us. And something amazing can happen. Those who show their love for us are blessed as we are blessed by their aid. The same thing happens when we help others in need. And there are so many people in need! We are blessed when we help them. And one way, one relatively easy, cost free way of helping people, is to pray for them, to ask God to bless them and protect them. I say relatively as I believe that as we gain experience in prayer, that cost grows – in terms of time spent and emotional energy expended. Yet there is a blessing for interceding before God for others. So, let us pray.

Father in heaven, thank you that you hear our prayers. While at times it may seem like the sky is bronze above us, you are listening. Bless you and thank you that you love us and care about our needs and the needs of others. As Jesus said, the birds and the flowers are provided for, will you not also provide for us. And you do! Please, help us in our uncertainty of

what to pray for. Guide us to pray in your will. Lead us to ask without selfish intent or greed, but out of love and concern and with your wisdom. May we become as fervent in praying for others as we are for our own needs. You tell us to ask, to seek, to knock — help us to continue and persevere in prayer, and give us faith to believe the answer is on its way. Amen

Day 20

Enough trouble

So do not worry, saying, 'What shall we eat?' or 'What shall we drink?' or 'What shall we wear?' For the pagans run after all these things, and your heavenly Father knows that you need them. But seek first his kingdom and his righteousness, and all these things will be given to you as well. Therefore do not worry about tomorrow, for tomorrow will worry about itself. Each day has enough trouble of its own.
Matthew 6:31-34

Each day has enough trouble. And so, Jesus makes it clear that following him will not prevent our daily troubles. Today has its troubles. Tomorrow will have trouble. We are advised by the one who loves us and knows exactly what troubles we are going through today and will go through tomorrow – to choose not to worry about tomorrow. And yet I do. Or at least, I have worried about tomorrow. I have known this whole time what troubles may face me tomorrow. It was too much for me, the knowledge of possible futures, the choices my daughter could make, the impact on her body, her health.

Unlike many whose child identifies as trans, I did not face daily battles with my child. Some reading this have decisions to make each day. Do you affirm or not affirm your child's trans identity? Do you use a new name or continue to refer to your child by the name you gave, or even choose a neutral name? Do you refer to your child with their preferred pronouns, continue to use the obvious pronouns based on their observed sexed body, or avoid pronouns at all? I have not had to face my child screaming at me, insulting me, being violent towards me. Some of you do face this. I have not had to deal with cross-dressing or secret use of cross-sex hormones. As an estranged parent I've been spared all that. Instead of immediate and in my face troubles I've been left with a void. In the Information Technology (IT) field where I work we might call this a Black Box – something we are aware of but do not understand, a system whose workings are unknown, processes hidden from us. Yet estrangement as I've experienced it is like a dark chasm, into which my child has fallen. I cannot see where she is, I don't know whether she is still alive or whether she is hurt or wounded. She may be wandering around down there, quite happy and content, or she may be curled up in a ball, afraid to even weep for fear of what might be listening and ready to pounce. This void of estrangement is one in which my fears have grown. I have found myself catastrophising worst case scenarios, cycling down into despair and depression. Without facts, without knowledge, my imagination has attempted to fill the gap. My imagination cannot be trusted.

When my wife challenged me on this recently, this set me thinking. Perhaps I should pray blessing into this void. Pray that our loving Father in heaven would fill this space, not for me, but for my child. Pray my child would have a sure foundation in Jesus Christ, that she would be led to build in her life that which would endure, the metaphorical gold and silver and precious jewels. Pray that our Father in heaven would build a room for her, both here on earth and in the promised Holy City, a place of beauty and worth, somewhere that she knows the peace of God, and where she can go out from to explore and adventure.

I do not know how I would handle what you have to deal with each day. I have had to deal with my own trouble. I have had to try and learn to give up again and again my fears and worries and doubts. Perhaps I have clung too closely to these, not having anything else. I have been afraid that if I stopped worrying it would be a sign I no longer cared, no longer loved my child. But has that been a lie from the evil one? Is it possible to be aware that things could become worse, and even having that knowledge to choose not to worry about the future?

Jesus was giving timeless advice. Do not worry. You may not have the food or drink or clothes you want and even need, yet your Father in heaven loves you and will provide if we ask him. Our needs, though not always our wants. A conversation with a good friend this week explored some thoughts I found useful to consider. Bad things happen because we do or do not do, because other people do or do not do. It may be that we do not have because we did not do what we needed to do or did something we should not have done. It may also be because others did not do, or they did what should not have been done. And billions of people on this planet, all doing and not doing and how can it be God's fault that what we wanted we did not get when there was always more than enough for everyone.

But Jesus' advice is far broader than worries about simple food and drink and clothing. What about our child? What about their mental health? About their physical health? Should we not worry about our children? Of course we must. What kind of parent would we be if we did not concern ourselves with our child's health? But a child becomes an adult and we must step back and allow them to make their own choices whether for good or for ill, and suffer the consequences if suffering is the consequence of their decision.

Pursue righteousness Jesus said — our Father's

righteousness. How does this help us? How does pursuing our Father's kingdom help us in and through this daily battle we face for and sometimes with our children? Look again at the words Jesus uses:

"But seek first his kingdom and his righteousness, and all these things will be given to you as well."

All these things will be given to you as well. Jesus tells us to seek God's kingdom and God's righteousness, yet it is not our seeking that gets us the kingdom or righteousness, no, these are both gifts from the Father to us, gifts as we saw when we explored the meaning of The Breastplate of Righteousness. And righteousness is a protection to us, as is being part of the kingdom of God. We are not alone in this fight for our children. God is fighting this battle for us. For today though I want to remind you of Jesus' advice to us – that we should ask God:

"Give us today our daily bread."
Matthew 6:11

And in this template for prayer – as I believe it is – does bread not stand for all the things we need? Whether bread, or water, clothes or shoes, the health of our child, delivery from trans. We are told to ask God for all these things and trust that God will provide. And God does provide each day. Perhaps not all that we want, not the whole portion of what we have asked for, but what we need that day. And the next day. And the next. And who knows, if we got all we asked for the first time we asked for it, then what would be left to ask for tomorrow? If all our troubles were resolved today, is it possible we would be bored tomorrow and go out looking for more trouble? I have a sneaking suspicion that deep inside many of us is the spirit of a toddler that won't stop poking a sibling. Perhaps that affronts you, that I would say such a thing when you are going through such pain just now. Yet this morning I read chapter 31 of the book of Deuteronomy and it was a challenge to me. A command to be strong and courageous, and then followed up with a warning that Israel would choose trouble instead of blessing. Sometimes we have trouble because we brought it on ourselves. Some of us may receive God's blessing today and still, in spite of that, go and bring more trouble into our lives tomorrow. May God lead us to avoid trouble that we can avoid, to restrain ourselves where to act or speak would invite trouble into our lives. And where trouble cannot be avoided, may we seek to follow the teaching of Jesus and trust that God will deliver us.

Father in heaven, thank you for your kindness to us, your recognition that we do have trouble in this world, in our lives. Thank you that you do not leave us to fend for ourselves, but offer your help. Please, provide for our needs. Especially, provide for our children, deliver them from evil, lead them into your blessing. Forgive us where we have brought trouble on ourselves and on others. Where we are able to make amends and resolve what we have broken, help us to do this. Where we cannot, Father, we ask for your mercy and grace and kindness to undo what we are helpless to change. Where others have brought trouble into our lives, forgive them and deliver us from that trouble. You tell us to even show love to our enemies. Give us your love so that we can do that. Amen

Day 21

Outside of time

"And now, compelled by the Spirit, I am going to Jerusalem, not knowing what will happen to me there. I only know that in every city the Holy Spirit warns me that prison and hardships are facing me. However, I consider my life worth nothing to me; my only aim is to finish the race and complete the task the Lord Jesus has given me—the task of testifying to the good news of God's grace.
Acts 20:22-24

I had an unusual conversation yesterday with a close friend. Somehow, we got on to talking about God's perspective on our lives as being outside of time. I feel it is relevant to our situation, to your situation, and I'd like to explore this with you today.

Twice in the Old Testament accounts God shows he is in control of time. During one of the battles for Canaan the sun stops for a whole day allowing the Israelites to conquer their enemy.

On the day the Lord gave the Amorites over to Israel, Joshua said to the Lord in the presence of Israel: "Sun, stand still over Gibeon, and you, moon, over the Valley of Aijalon."
So the sun stood still, and the moon stopped, till the nation avenged itself on its enemies, as it is written in the Book of Jashar. The sun stopped in the middle of the sky and delayed going down about a full day.
Joshua 10:12-13

Many hundreds of years later King Hezekiah is offered a sign from God and a shadow moves backwards.

> *Hezekiah had asked Isaiah, "What will be the sign that the Lord will heal me and that I will go up to the temple of the Lord on the third day from now?"*
> *Isaiah answered, "This is the Lord's sign to you that the Lord will do what he has promised: Shall the shadow go forward ten steps, or shall it go back ten steps?"*
> *"It is a simple matter for the shadow to go forward ten steps," said Hezekiah. "Rather, have it go back ten steps."*
> *Then the prophet Isaiah called on the Lord, and the Lord made the shadow go back the ten steps it had gone down on the stairway of Ahaz.*
> *2 Kings 20:8-11*

I'm fascinated by these accounts and hope to integrate them into a novel one day. Was this what our science fiction writers would call time travel, or a manipulation of our solar system that would make most scientists quake in fear if they observed it? Perhaps you have seen the 1937 black and white movie: The Man Who Could Work Miracles. At the end of the movie, the miracle worker stops the rotation of the earth. However, everything loose continues to travel at the speed it was previously rotating around the Earth, including the air, causing utter destruction. Some mock the Biblical accounts above for this reason. Yet, these were clearly miracles and why should it be that God could not so arrange things that the earth came to a smooth halt in its rotation and even reversed for a time? I believe these events did happen and as a result, this indicates to me just how little we

Day 21: Outside of time

understand both about God and about this universe. For if God can cause the rotation of our planet to stop and even reverse, this indicates that nothing God chooses to do is impossible. And as I write this, I am convicted. I know of these accounts. I say I believe they happened, yet how little faith do I have to believe God could and will act today in such a miraculous manner. God forgive me.

But what if it was not a physical change to the Earth's rotation? We are not told how these accounts came about, only that they did. We know time is no obstacle to our God who shares through his prophets what will happen. The books of Daniel and Revelation in particular contain detailed and specific insight into events that had not happened when the prophecy was given, but have happened since. Even the books of the Torah, the accounts of Moses, prophesy that Israel will rebel against God and be taken into captivity. How could God know that unless he is outside of what we know as time.

Would you like to know what will happen to your child? What the outcome of their journey along the trans super-highway will be? Are you sure? I have asked God for revelation, though I'm not sure I honestly wanted an answer. What if the outcome is one that would crush us? What if our child, against all reason, and persuasion on our part, and despite endless prayers, chooses a path that is destructive? What good would it do us to know that in advance?

Tales of time travel tend to take only a few types. Either events can be changed or they cannot. If we have seen the future, does this mean the future is inevitable, or does it mean that future can be altered? Perhaps both possibilities are true at different times and for different reasons. I believe that prophecy is often given so that people will change their ways, and there are numerous examples of

God delaying punishment and even wiping the slate clean when people repent. Yet sometimes prophecy is given so that we are forewarned and will not lose faith when the worst happens. Paul was warned through prophecy that if he went to Jerusalem he would be bound:

> **After we had been there a number of days, a prophet named Agabus came down from Judea. Coming over to us, he took Paul's belt, tied his own hands and feet with it and said, "The Holy Spirit says, 'In this way the Jewish leaders in Jerusalem will bind the owner of this belt and will hand him over to the Gentiles.'" When we heard this, we and the people there pleaded with Paul not to go up to Jerusalem. Then Paul answered, "Why are you weeping and breaking my heart? I am ready not only to be bound, but also to die in Jerusalem for the name of the Lord Jesus." When he would not be dissuaded, we gave up and said, "The Lord's will be done."**
> **Acts 21:10-14**

If I recall correctly, in the months after our daughter revealed her trans identity, several people asked me – what if this was God's will? I felt then and still feel that was a cruel thing to say to a parent. What if it is God's will your child will suffer? How can that ever be God's will? Yet children do suffer, as we as parents also suffer. If suffering is not in God's will then why do we suffer. And back to the conversation with my friend – We agreed that bad things happen because we ourselves act to make them happen, or because other people act to make them happen. Or even because we or they have not acted. Not every bad thing has a direct human cause. An earthquake likely does not happen because I did something, though perhaps on occasion what appear to be natural events do have their roots in some sinful behaviour or spiritual influence. Jesus warned against assuming all such events are the result of sin. But a nation can be judged. We have the destruction of the tribes of Canaan as an early example of judgement. Jonah's prophecy against Nineveh – and that especially is worth dwelling on. Jonah prophesied the consequences of that nation's sin would be utter destruction, and their response was to repent, and because they repented, God postponed the destruction. An example of sharing the future with people and people choosing a different path which meant that future did not happen, at least for them.

Paul was warned of his probable arrest and the hardships he would face. Knowing that the good news of Jesus would be preached as a result of that, he was willing to face the suffering that had been prophesied. This is the same Paul who wrote to the people who would imprison and ultimately execute him:

And we know that in all things God works for the good of those who love him, who have been called according to his purpose.
Romans 8:28

Was it good for Paul to suffer in this way? Earlier in his letter he had written:

Not only so, but we also glory in our sufferings, because we know that suffering produces perseverance; perseverance, character; and character, hope. And hope does not put us to shame, because God's love has been poured out into our hearts through the Holy Spirit, who has been given to us.
Romans 5:3-5

Paul had a God's eye perspective on suffering. Many of our children, caught up in trans, either are suffering or will suffer due to following the false teaching that they "must" take puberty blockers, "must" take cross-sex hormones, "must" have surgery. They will not be suffering to cause the good news of Jesus to be shared. I believe that for all our children, it would be better for them if they desisted or detransitioned from their trans identity. I believe the concept of a trans identity is based on many lies. To attempt to live a life based on such lies is unhealthy and dangerous even if no drugs are taken or surgeries had. Perhaps our role as parents is to prophesy to our children, to ask God what we should say, how we should say it, when we should say it so that our children will be warned and perhaps, like those in Nineveh, we will see our children repent and desist.

However, if they do not desist, or do not desist in time to prevent irreversible damage to themselves, it may be that God can even take that evil and in the end use it for the good of our child, use their suffering even though it would have been better for everyone had they not suffered. God alone knows what will happen. Let us keep asking him to save our children and for his wisdom to know what we should say to them and when.

Father in heaven, you alone know the future, you alone know the choices our children will make and what the outcome will be. Rescue our children. Deliver them from the false beliefs they have. Give us your wisdom and discernment and courage to warn our children. May their eyes be opened to see the truth, may their ears be opened to hear the truth, may their hearts and minds be prepared to receive the truth. Give us faith to believe that you are the God who made this world, who caused it to spin and caused the sun to stand still and even go backwards. Give us faith to trust you and trust that you will answer our prayers for our children. Since you will not violate their free will, may they truly have free will and be set free from the lies they have believed and be set free from the hold that trans has on them. If the worst should happen, or a series of worsts, comfort us and fill us with the knowledge that you love our children, despite their bad decisions. Help us to continue to love them too. Amen

Day 22

Speaking up

"Son of man, I have made you a watchman for the people of Israel; so hear the word I speak and give them warning from me. When I say to a wicked person, 'You will surely die,' and you do not warn them or speak out to dissuade them from their evil ways in order to save their life, that wicked person will die for their sin, and I will hold you accountable for their blood. But if you do warn the wicked person and they do not turn from their wickedness or from their evil ways, they will die for their sin;
but you will have saved yourself.
Ezekiel 3:17-19

It is one thing to warn your community of an external threat, quite another to warn them of danger from within. If your community, or family, or company, or group has appointed you as their watchman, you would expect them to listen to you. It is a sad truth though that even when someone has been entrusted with such a task, occasionally they are ignored when warning challenges laziness, greed, or the holding of power. Internal danger is danger within the camp. I've been reading through Leviticus and am now into the book of Numbers. Repeated again and again is this instruction to put danger outside of the camp. The Israelites were to recognise threat, in the form of uncleanness, of infection, of sin that corrupts, and separate themselves from it, to maintain their relationship with their Holy God, to avoid risk of judgement:

The Lord said to Moses, "Command the Israelites to send away from the camp anyone who has a defiling skin disease or a discharge of any kind, or who is ceremonially unclean because of a dead body. Send away male and female alike; send them outside the camp so they will not defile their camp, where I dwell among them." The Israelites did so; they sent them outside the camp. They did just as the Lord had instructed Moses.
Numbers 5:1-4

I have observed so many large organisations display affirmation for trans identity. These organisations invite activist groups like Stonewall and Mermaids inside their camp to teach their employees. And what are they teaching their employees – you, your colleagues?

- They are teaching you to use a person's preferred pronouns – a form of gaslighting.
- They are teaching you to affirm your colleagues trans identity, and worse, to affirm your child's trans identity – without any warning of the risks and dangers.
- In some wealthier companies they may even have persuaded the employer to provide gender affirmation medical insurance – thereby risking future lawsuits and reputational damage.

I find myself asking – when will an employee or worker at one of these organisations sue the organisation for leading them to do something they have later regretted? And if such a lawsuit occurs and is successful, will hundreds and thousands of similar lawsuits be taken out?

Day 22: Speaking up

This is speculation on my part, but it concerns me and so for over a year now I have been raising concerns at my workplace. I have been speaking up because I do not want the blood of my colleagues on my head. In my community, I want to know I have warned of the danger.

But it has been difficult. I know too many awful consequences and my tendency to catastrophise causes me to have to be very careful about what I share. Yet this is one situation where it may be that those who can see the worst case scenario may be the ones that need listened to.

I feel that those companies that promote Pride and LGBTQ+ without systematic analysis of what is being promoted, are taking on an unknown risk which could prove very costly, even if no lawsuits related to harm caused from gender affirming surgery are taken out. If a colleague of mine submits to a castration procedure under a companies medical insurance, and later regrets it, what would be the fallout from that? Certainly loss of trust. Resentment. Bitterness. Anger. And on the side of those who encouraged and celebrated the decision – now regretted – shame and guilt.

Will colleagues continue to hold in high regard those who led another colleague to castrate themselves or remove their breasts, operations which cannot be undone? What will that do to morale within the organisation?

And worse, in my view – far, far worse – what about those organisations that have encouraged colleagues who are parents to lead their children down a dark and dangerous path? I know the anger I feel as a parent, as a father against those who have "only" affirmed my daughter's trans identity . I'm unsure any leader at any of these organisations who promote Pride and LGBTQ+ understand quite the reputational or financial risk they may have inadvertently taken on board.

It is a difficult thing to speak up against the crowd. But you can ask questions. Asking questions like:

- Have you read the recommendations of the Cass Report?
- Since the leak of the WPATH Files has brought that organisation into disrepute, would this indicate that following WPATH guidance is something that should be reviewed?
- You state that your companies' policies are inclusive and diverse, does this include those who have rejected a trans identity and now are desisting from that trans identity?
- You have promoted the stories of individuals who identify as trans, when will you promote the stories of those who have detransitioned?
- Is it ethical to promote castration as a form of gender affirmative surgery when this cannot be reversed?
- Is there a risk of bringing the company into reputational disrepute and/or lawsuits being taken out against the company for giving advice to affirm trans identified children and/or colleagues when the Cass report indicates this is a non-neutral act and there is only poor-quality evidence suggesting we should affirm?

These are just a few pointed questions that all of us should be free to ask. I know from my own situation that while no company should retaliate against someone for asking reasonable questions, and trying to help protect a company from risk, that raising these questions has been extremely stressful. Yet I do not want to be known as someone who stayed silent, who did nothing, while others were harmed. May you have wisdom and courage to speak up in ways that will help others to understand the dangers associated with trans affirming treatments.

Father in heaven, thank you that you warn us, that you sent your prophets and eventually your son to tell us of the dangers we face from disobeying you, from rejecting you, from sinning against others. Give us the courage and wisdom and discernment we need to warn others. Cause their ears to be opened and their eyes to see. May those that lie and deceive be exposed. May those who have believed the lies be set free and enabled to understand the risks from pursuing gender affirmative "treatments". May those who have been harmed already find healing and comfort in you. Amen

Day 23 — Wolves in sheep's clothing

"Watch out for false prophets. They come to you in sheep's clothing, but inwardly they are ferocious wolves. By their fruit you will recognize them. Do people pick grapes from thornbushes, or figs from thistles?
Matthew 7:15-16

While we were still reeling from our child's identification as trans and the response of some in our family, a family member met someone who offered to help. Without our knowledge this person asked to speak with our children, and afterwards offered to meet with us. This person was introduced to us as someone who had been very helpful, a fellow Christian, someone who had experience of helping families in our "situation". When I found out this person had spoken to our older children, I was concerned. Our older children were adults, they can and could speak to whomever they wanted, yet I found myself interpreting this as a red flag. I felt we had no choice but to see him, if only to check him out.

He told us he charged a nominal amount for his "counselling" or "therapy". After a brief phone call I was still extremely wary, but felt we should meet with him in person, after all it was probably better to find out more about this person who was having conversations with our children. He turned up one afternoon and we welcomed him into our house. He told us a little bit about himself and asked us to share our story. And then he responded to some of the things we were saying and I felt a familiar sensation that I'd experienced before. An uneasiness in my spirit that was like a tugging in my gut.

I don't get such sensations often, and usually when I do I am unsure whether it is a "spiritual" sign, or just a stomach ache, or maybe a natural intuition – though it may be possible that what we sometimes interpret as intuition may be a prompt from God. John in his first letter advises this:

> ***Dear friends, do not believe every spirit, but test the spirits to see whether they are from God, because many false prophets have gone out into the world. This is how you can recognize the Spirit of God: Every spirit that acknowledges that Jesus Christ has come in the flesh is from God, but every spirit that does not acknowledge Jesus is not from God. This is the spirit of the antichrist, which you have heard is coming and even now is already in the world.***
> ***1 John 4:1-3***

At that time, in that moment, I wasn't conscious of a need to test any spirit. In good faith, we'd welcomed this man into our home hoping he might be able to help us reconcile with our children. I was attempting to hold my reservations cautiously, allowing him a chance to prove himself trustworthy. Yet as the session went on, he didn't seem to really be listening to us and I tried to explain my perspective in a different way. It was as if he had a script, or a perspective on our situation that he wanted to impose on us. He'd had experience with someone coming out as trans before, he said. He'd helped the parents on that journey, he said. From how he described it, it sounded like the only journey he could envisage was one of us affirming our child's trans identity. I wasn't able to process it all fast

Day 23: Wolves in sheep's clothing

enough but was conscious at some level that he felt he should be in control, in charge of this situation and he seemed a little frustrated that I wasn't just accepting his guidance.

After we'd shared for some time and my wife had become emotional, he asked if he could sit next to my wife. I seem to remember asking him why he wanted to do this. In all honesty I didn't trust him. And I was conflicted because it is quite common in Christian circles for people to sit next to people and offer to pray for them and this person had been introduced as a Christian by a family member that we trusted, with what Christians call a "ministry" – a God given talent or gift for helping people. So reluctantly I agreed he could sit next to my wife. Then he asked to hold her hand and again I questioned him as to why. I felt conflicted even as I asked this reasonable question. Who was this strange man wanting to hold my wife's hand? That was another level of intimacy – closer than sitting next to my wife – but I couldn't think fast enough or explain why I felt so resistant to what he was asking. Then he asked if he could blow on her. I said no. Loudly and assertively. Unbelievably he actually dared to question me at my refusal – telling me that I had no right to tell my wife what she could do, that if she wanted him to blow on her I had no business saying that couldn't happen. I told him this needed to stop. Now!

I don't know what he heard or saw but he immediately stood and put on his jacket, making as if to go. I didn't understand what had just happened and an innate hospitality drive kicked in. I told him he didn't have to go but he insisted. I said I'd pay him for his time and I admit, there was a part of me thinking that if I did pay him then I'd have a legal right to sue him. But he insisted on leaving and I watched him drive away, then went in and essentially said to my wife — what just happened?

It took us both a few days to process the experience. We ended up separately writing down our recollections of meeting this person. It didn't take me all that long to decide he was a wolf wearing a very clever disguise. Someone who preyed on vulnerable people and ignored normal safeguarding advice. He had the audacity to question our feelings and concerns when a professional would have had the sense to listen and try and understand. He tried to tell us what we should expect even though nobody can say what will or will not happen when a child decides they are trans. He gave the appearance of being spiritual, but I'm glad that as a husband I drew a line and told him no. Perhaps the final straw for me was the risk of my wife being subject to a spiritual influence from him blowing on her. There is a scene in the bible when Jesus breathes on his disciples and tells them to receive his spirit. But if the Holy Spirit of Jesus can be imparted through breathing on a person, is it also possible that an evil spirit could be so imparted? I did not want to risk that for my wife.

My wife's view is much more generous. Was he simply unwise, perhaps had never had someone question him or his views? And I could simply delete all I had written about him if not for one last thought — what if the Devil was using him to lead us to affirm our child and he was not the wolf, but was the sheep's clothing?

We've never spoken to this person since, nor heard from him or of him. It does concern me that he may still be out there, putting himself forward as someone who can help, yet possibly making situations worse. He gave the impression of believing that we needed to affirm our child, that affirmation was the only possible way to reconciliation and in that he may have been right. However, I don't

Day 23: Wolves in sheep's clothing

believe that reconciliation should require me to lie, or should come at the cost of my child suffering for the rest of her life. I've met other people on this journey who have said similar things, who have indicated I am at fault for my unwillingness to affirm the trans identity. How can I when I see no evidence it is based in reality? When I see evidence that some desist from that identity?

Jesus warns us to watch out for false prophets, for those who are a wolf in the clothing of a sheep. Listen to your intuition, to your gut feelings, do not ignore them. Your intuition and gut feeling may be the way God is warning you of danger, that someone cannot be trusted.

Father in heaven, thank you that you warn us of danger, that you have given us both natural and supernatural instincts. Give us your discernment to warn us of those who cannot be trusted. Help us to trust your warnings. You also warn us not to trust our hearts as our hearts can be led astray. Where we have feelings or perceptions that are incorrect, where we have misinterpreted danger where there is none, may you guide us to understand that. And Father, please give our children your discernment. If they listen to you they will be saved from much pain and suffering. Guide them and speak to them that they will be led away from danger and back to you. Amen

Day 24

Twenty years

This was my situation: The heat consumed me in the daytime and the cold at night, and sleep fled from my eyes. It was like this for the twenty years I was in your household. I worked for you fourteen years for your two daughters and six years for your flocks, and you changed my wages ten times. If the God of my father, the God of Abraham and the Fear of Isaac, had not been with me, you would surely have sent me away empty-handed. But God has seen my hardship and the toil of my hands, and last night he rebuked you."
Genesis 31:40-42

Will I ever see my children again? Will they reconcile with me? These questions are never far from my thoughts. I'm aware there are parents who have suffered estrangement for far longer than I have – at time of writing two and a half years. Many others have not been estranged and instead have long suffered through a difficult relationship with their trans identified child. Some parents have written about having to live with the situation for a decade or more. I was reminded this morning that Jacob – who was eventually given the name Israel – left his parents and worked away from his family for fourteen years. At that time there was no Internet, no phone network, not even a postal service. Messages could have been sent by courier though there is no record of Jacob ever writing home. Then, when I looked up the passage in the book of Genesis I found he wasn't away from his parents for fourteen years, he was away for twenty!

Twenty years. Two decades. Enough time to have a child and raise them to adulthood. That is a lifetime. A lifetime with no contact from your child. There is a part of me that understands that is what I may face. My children are all adults now and have chosen to walk their own path. If that path never leads back to me, then it is possible that no matter how much time I have left, it will be without them in my life. Understanding is not the same as accepting. I am trying to give this up to God. I have attempted to relinquish them to God, let go of them and trust God will guide them. I suspect this may be a process, may be something I need to do many times. Perhaps I will find there are layers of relinquishment.

I could not remember whether Jacob saw his parents again. When I checked, I found this:

> **Jacob came home to his father Isaac in Mamre, near Kiriath Arba (that is, Hebron), where Abraham and Isaac had stayed. Isaac lived a hundred and eighty years. Then he breathed his last and died and was gathered to his people, old and full of years. And his sons Esau and Jacob buried him.**
> **Genesis 35:27-29**

So, after twenty years, Isaac did see his son Jacob once more. I cannot see though when Jacob's mother died. Her death does not appear to be recorded. Did she live to see her son return? Perhaps not. It is a fact that some children never return. Even those who part on good terms might emigrate to the other side of the world, or just up the road yet live a life as distant from us parents as if they were half a planet away.

The story of Jacob's departure from his parents has themes that will be familiar to many with trans identifying

Day 24: Twenty years

children, those of deceit and betrayal. One parent conspired with the child to deceive the other parent. One child betrayed the other, dressing up in their clothes and applying their scent to attempt to pass themselves as that child. One parent betrayed. One child betrayed. How many parents have been as shaken as Isaac was when he learned of the betrayal, as angry as Esau was to find his brother had stolen his birthright? Yes, in this case Jacob did not attempt to pretend to be a different sex, yet I do find the parallels are striking.

My child has taken a new name, many of our children have, though it is not at all clear to me that my child's new name is from God. Our names are important, perhaps more important than we realise. Jacob is forever known as the deceiver. Yet despite his deceit, despite his betrayal, his father blessed him and gave him advice when he left. And God watched over him. And eventually Jacob acknowledged that God had protected him and provided for him. And God then gives him a new name. A name that speaks of strength and resilience, a name that shows a willingness to stand up even to God: Israel.

If Isaac had not blessed Jacob, history may have been cut short right there. Israel may never have existed. The royal line leading to Jesus may have been broken. Did God have a back-up plan? Or maybe I am catastrophising? Even if Isaac had not blessed Jacob, perhaps God would have still followed him, protected him and made him into the great nation of Israel. Yet Isaac did bless his son. The son who deceived him, who betrayed him. And that encourages me that we can do the same – bless our children even though they have deceived or betrayed us.

My prayer for my child, for all my children, is that they will return to the God of their father. That God will protect them as he did me. That God will provide for them and guide them as he has done for me. If I must wait ten years or twenty years or a lifetime and never see them again, then may God do what I cannot and guide my children so that eventually they will also one day say that they belong to God.

Father in heaven, thank you for my children. They have been and are still a blessing to me and I am grateful to you for the gift they have been. While I am distressed at their choices, I ask you to bless them and guide them as you blessed and guided Jacob. Watch over them and lead them. Lead them to one day recognise that you are in their lives and always have been. Lead them to see your miraculous provision and know it can only have come from you. Protect them from harm and danger and from those who would cheat and deceive them. Bless my children, Father, and I thank you that you will. Amen

Day 25

Plan to prosper

This is what the Lord Almighty, the God of Israel, says to all those I carried into exile from Jerusalem to Babylon: "Build houses and settle down; plant gardens and eat what they produce. Marry and have sons and daughters; find wives for your sons and give your daughters in marriage, so that they too may have sons and daughters. Increase in number there; do not decrease. Also, seek the peace and prosperity of the city to which I have carried you into exile. Pray to the Lord for it, because if it prospers, you too will prosper."
Jeremiah 29:4-7

For those taken captive from Israel into Babylon, this may have been a difficult instruction to hear. I know that I was conscious from the start that I could be facing a long road ahead when I found out my daughter identified as trans. For some families it can take up to a decade before the child realises or admits they were mistaken. For others, there is no end. They will not live to see their child repent of their decision. Israel was to spend seventy years in captivity, their punishment for hundreds of years of disobedience, of failure to observe the Sabbath Years as commanded in Leviticus 25.

In the law given to Moses, every seventh year was to be a year where no planting was done, no harvest was taken. God promised that he would provide miraculously for his people, yet as each seventh year rolled round, Israel failed to trust their God and continued to plant and harvest as before. At the very end of the book of 2 Chronicles we are told that seventy Sabbath Years were not honoured and so the land was to rest from the ceaseless production of food.

Can we as parents learn something from this? It is possible that I need to learn to let my children be. To give them rest from my questions, my prompting, my interference in their lives. I need to give my children a Sabbath, perhaps many Sabbath years, and to allow God to gently and gradually restore them? If so, then this word given by the prophet Jeremiah to the exiles may be relevant to those of us as parents who need to step back from our children – or as in my case, who are currently estranged.

You do not build a house and settle down if you are in it for the short term. You do not plant gardens unless you plan to be there for harvest. A few years ago I was afraid. I read the news, watched reports of terrible events, doom and gloom and the end of the world. I found myself convicted that God wanted me to plan for the future. I was to invest for the long term. Settle down, put down roots. My attitude gradually changed and instead of worrying about the future, I began to prepare for a better life. To repair our home, to look to sell it and buy a more expensive property, to risk taking out a larger mortgage. Those years since have seen us prosper financially, yet at the same time, I have found myself estranged from my children. Would it have been better had I not moved house? Had I been content where I was? I don't know. I do believe that word to plan and prepare and invest was from God. I also know that those who seek to obey God will face troubles and persecutions and suffering. So perhaps I should not be surprised that as some things have gone well, others things have gone terribly.

Our children are precious to us. They are our future. Each of us will eventually die and we hope our children

Day 25: Plan to prosper

will live on, that they will have families of their own and children to carry on our name and our line. Trans – in my view – is a curse on a family. As children take puberty blockers and cross-sex hormones, they risk being sterilised. It is not possible for anyone to change sex and so the child who submits to surgery is not replacing one set of sex organs with another, but instead is losing the only functioning sexual organs they can ever have. There are many reasons I oppose trans ideology. This is one of the most wicked aspects – to take away from a young person the ability to ever have children.

It can destroy a parent to know their child has done this to themselves, that they plan to do this to themselves. Yet our loving Father in heaven does not want us as parents to destroy ourselves. We may go through a long period of mourning, may return again and again to times of grief. Yet despite the terrible situation we find our family in, I am sure that our Father will eventually want us to begin to build and plant again. To invest in our future. For some of us even perhaps have more children.

Even though the land was to rest, even if we are to let our children be, our Father still has a plan for our lives, cares about our future. And as the prophet instructed, we should always continue to seek peace and prosperity for our children and our society. It may be that our children will return to God and to us. May this be. And we live in this society whether we like it or not. If this society prospers, then we too will prosper.

Father in heaven, thank you for my child, for all my children. Thank you that you gave them to me, that you blessed me with them. Please protect them from harm and prevent them from further harming themselves. Place a shield around them, a hedge of protection. Lead them back to you. You are kind, showing mercy and grace to sinners and those who rebelled against you. Show again your great mercy and grace by rescuing my children, delivering them from the path to destruction. And Father, please work in our country to turn the hearts and minds of those who lead us against this evil ideology, to legislate that no-one will be allowed to give cross-sex hormones, or drugs to block puberty, or perform so-called gender affirming surgeries; that women and girls are protected from the invasion of their private spaces by males, that their achievements are no longer stolen by men who identify as trans. Amen

Day 26 — If her father had spit in her face

*So Moses cried out to the Lord,
"Please, God, heal her!"
The Lord replied to Moses, "If her father had spit in her face, would she not have been in disgrace for seven days? Confine her outside the camp for seven days; after that she can be brought back." So Miriam was confined outside the camp for seven days, and the people did not move on till she was brought back.
Numbers 12:13-15*

Reading the above passage this week I was taken aback by this statement. For over a couple of years now I have been punishing myself. Blaming myself for the breakdown in relationships with my children. I still believe I may have to apologise to each of them. Still need to humble myself to enable reconciliation. Yet this passage gave me a different perspective. We live in a culture that disobeys this primary commandment of God:

*"Honor your father and your mother, so that you may live long in the land the Lord your God is giving you.
Exodus 20:12*

The older I get, the more conscious I am of my own failings in honouring my parents. I look back on how I treated them as a child, as a teenager and then a young man and see so many parallels with how my own children treat me today. The Cat's in the cradle as the song goes. I think I have heard it said this is the only commandment with a promise, though that is not the case. Look back through Exodus 20 and we see this:

"You shall not make for yourself an image in the form of anything in heaven above or on the earth beneath or in the waters below. You shall not bow down to them or worship them; for I, the Lord your God, am a jealous God, punishing the children for the sin of the parents to the third and fourth generation of those who hate me, but showing love to a thousand generations of those who love me and keep my commandments.
Exodus 20:4-6

There is a promise here – that the Lord will show love to a thousand generations of those who love him and keep his commandments. That is quite some promise! And seeing that, the command to honour one's father and mother has much more force. If our parents have honoured the Lord, and we honour them, we will also seek to follow their example by honouring their God – our God. And in so doing, we will reap the blessing promised including a long life in the promised land.

But what for those children who do not honour their parents, who turn away from the commands of their parents' God? Do they receive the blessing promised to the children of parents who honoured the Lord? Perhaps. Perhaps they will be blessed despite having done nothing to deserve it. Maybe they will enjoy a long life, will receive the love of God. Though I suspect there is a great difference between those who receive God's love in spite of their rejection of God and those who receive his love, continuing to honour both God and their parents.

I believe the two commands together show how a

nation can prosper. If the young respect the old, listen to them, learn from them, receive the wisdom the old have to offer, then the young will benefit from the wisdom and teaching given. If the young have contempt for the old, refuse to listen to advice and warnings, it is likely things will not end well. I know, sometimes those of us who are older fail to see opportunity and recognise a need for change. Sometimes the young are given blessings that are strange and unusual to those of us who are older. Yet some wisdom and advice is timeless, always applicable, and it is a wise youth who realises that early.

My thinking changed this week as I read God's judgement of Miriam. She had sinned against Moses and in doing so had sinned against God. Miriam was to be sent outside the camp for seven days. Why? Because she was unclean. She was unclean because God had judged her, punished her. Our culture doesn't like stories like this – God punishing someone. For what? For complaining! Does God still do that? Punish those who complain? Yes, I believe he does. How often have I complained? That is a question that pulled me up as I thought about this account. It is worth reading the whole chapter. It is also worth reading all the way through from Exodus and into Numbers! And how will God punish our children who have rejected us, rejected our teaching, our advice, who do not honour us, do not respect us? Well, perhaps God will give them what they desire. Would that not be punishment enough. If they want a life without God, perhaps God will give them that. If they want to cut off healthy body parts, perhaps God will allow them to do that. If they want to take dangerous drugs and chemical cocktails, perhaps God will allow that. And so our children will reap in their bodies and their lives all that they desire only to find that what they desired was a pit they dug for themselves. A trap they will have to spend the rest of their lives in.

> *The anger of the Lord burned against them, and he left them. When the cloud lifted from above the tent, Miriam's skin was leprous—it became as white as snow. Aaron turned toward her and saw that she had a defiling skin disease, and he said to Moses, "Please, my lord, I ask you not to hold against us the sin we have so foolishly committed. Do not let her be like a stillborn infant coming from its mother's womb with its flesh half eaten away."*
> *So Moses cried out to the Lord,*
> *"Please, God, heal her!"*
> *Numbers 12:9-13*

If you read the whole account, you find that Aaron asked Moses for forgiveness for Miriam and Moses cried out to God for her. I am sure any of you reading this who have children identifying as trans have cried out to God for them. I certainly have for my children. Yet Miriam was punished and worse – she had to bear the shame of being sent outside the camp for seven days, the same as any other who had an infectious skin disease. And in God's response to Moses, God indicated his contempt for her. "If her father had spit in her face"! I would never spit in my child's face, yet was this a cultural action? I think I've seen people from other cultures today spit as a sign of contempt.

Thinking about this as the day went on, I felt that as a father I need to recognise the authority God has given me. Not that I need or want to spit in my child's face, but that God expects children to honour their parents. And God honours parents. And as parents, as a father, I do have authority – even a limited authority over my adult children.

I have authority to speak up and act in my child's best interests. I have authority to defend my vulnerable child, a young adult who currently appears incapable of questioning her own decisions, and deciding whether the long term risks outweigh the perceived benefits. Our relationship has changed, will continue to change over time, yet it is not ultimately us who will suffer if our children fail to obey God's command to honour their parents, it is they who will suffer. I have authority to bless. I may even have authority to curse though may God keep me from doing that. I will continue to love them and pray for them and hope to be reconciled with them. But God is not expecting me to humiliate myself before them. Humble myself, yes, but our culture seems to want parents to be humiliated. Our children often have contempt for us. Enough! It is time for us parents to recognise our God given authority.

Father in heaven, thank you for my parents, thank you for the blessing they were to me, giving me the gift of life. Thank you for my children. Thank you for the blessing they are to me. Where my children have sinned against me, lead them to repentance. Where they have dishonoured me, lead them to see they have not only sinned against me but also against you. Please have mercy on them. It may be that nothing will get through to them but the consequences of their sin, just as Miriam suffered as the result of her complaints against your servant. Yet even towards Miriam you showed mercy. Please show mercy towards my children and allow them to know and understand your kindness to them. Give me strength and wisdom to recognise the authority you have placed in me and to act in that authority. Amen

Day 27

In your anger do not sin

Then Moses became very angry and said to the Lord, "Do not accept their offering. I have not taken so much as a donkey from them, nor have I wronged any of them."
Numbers 16:15

I have been so, so angry. Angry enough to curse. Angry enough to ask God to punish. I don't know, I cannot know what it is like for you, to have a child identify as trans, to be verbally assaulted day after day, perhaps to be physically attacked by your child because you will not submit to their will. Perhaps to have other family, neighbours, people you thought were your friends all gaslight you and try and convince you to ignore your instincts, to attempt to put out of your mind the thought of risk, of future problems, of danger. To have them try and make you forget, if such a thing was possible, that you once read evidence suggesting none of it is real.

I've been angry. I know this and have been fighting with my anger for years now. Sometimes having some victory, sometimes so consumed by the fury inside me that I can barely think.

As I've read through the account of Moses I've seen his patience tested again and again. So many times he stood between God and the Israelites. God's anger ready to wipe them out and start over, yet Moses was there, interceding for them, pleading for them. And yet Moses was human – just like us. Moses got angry, just like us. And sometimes even the ever patient Moses had had enough. Numbers 16 is a stunning read. How could the Israelites have forgotten or ignored all that had just happened? Only a short time before, the whole community had listened to a majority of spies who told them effectively that they could not trust God. That the same God who had wiped out the Egyptian army was incapable of fighting on their behalf against the people of Canaan. Those spies were executed for their treason against God. Executed by whom? By God, through a plague. A plague. Every adult there must have been able to remember the ten plagues of Egypt. It had only been a couple of years previously at most. Plagues were sent as punishment. And yet still the people of Israel did not listen. Some of them at least. 250 of them got so riled up that they began spreading false rumours against Moses and Aaron. And Moses' patience finally broke. He became angry as we read in the passage above.

He then may have repented of his anger. Certainly, Moses seems to have a bit of an emotional roller-coaster going on. At one point he tells God not to accept the offering of the people, the next moment he is again interceding for their protection.

Jesus warns us against anger in his famous sermon on the mount.

"You have heard that it was said to the people long ago, 'You shall not murder, and anyone who murders will be subject to judgement.' But I tell you that anyone who is angry with a brother or sister will be subject to judgement. Again, anyone who says to a brother or sister, 'Raca,' is answerable to the court. And anyone who says, 'You fool!' will be in danger of the fire of hell."
Matthew 5:21-22

Such a simple statement Jesus makes – anyone who is angry with their brother or sister will be subject to judgement. Anyone. You, me, anyone who is angry is subject to judgement.

The Lord said to Moses, "Take the staff, and you and your brother Aaron gather the assembly together. Speak to that rock before their eyes and it will pour out its water. You will bring water out of the rock for the community so they and their livestock can drink." So Moses took the staff from the Lord's presence, just as he commanded him. He and Aaron gathered the assembly together in front of the rock and Moses said to them, "Listen, you rebels, must we bring you water out of this rock?" Then Moses raised his arm and struck the rock twice with his staff. Water gushed out, and the community and their livestock drank.
But the Lord said to Moses and Aaron, "Because you did not trust in me enough to honour me as holy in the sight of the Israelites, you will not bring this community into the land I give them."
Numbers 20:7-12

As I read the account above, it is not stated specifically that Moses was angry, yet that is what I read. Moses anger, leading him to contempt for his people, leading him to ignore the Lord's clear instruction to speak to the rock and instead he – angrily – strikes the rock with his staff. Maybe I am wrong. Maybe my interpretation is incorrect. God's judgement of Moses refers to his lack of trust. And maybe Moses was masking his doubts – would God honour him if he only spoke to the rock? The staff had been used before to bring about a miracle, maybe he should put his trust in that and not in God? That certainly appears to have been the case. Yet I see anger in Moses – and perhaps I am seeing my anger there, not the anger of Moses. I am interpreting his actions in light of how I might have felt or behaved. And if so, then please forgive me.

I feel that I must speak to myself about anger. Must share this with you. Because I am reminded of this teaching:

> **Therefore each of you must put off falsehood and speak truthfully to your neighbour, for we are all members of one body. "In your anger do not sin": Do not let the sun go down while you are still angry, and do not give the devil a foothold.**
> **Ephesians 4:25-27**

In your anger, do not sin. Any of us may become angry at any time. I believe there is much to be angry about. Yet I would spare you the consequences of your anger. I would spare myself the judgement that my anger might bring about. Perhaps we need to sacrifice our anger – bring it to God, and trust, trust that God will save us, and our child.

Father in heaven, anger is an emotion you have given us. I thank you for the gift of anger which can be used effectively when it is under control. Yet I know that all too often I have not been in control of my anger. I have spoken words I now regret, shouted words that should not have been uttered. Please forgive me for the times I have let my anger control me and when my anger has led me into sin. I suspect I will be angry again, how can I not be angry when there is so much evil affecting my family. Caution me by your Holy Spirit to restrain my anger and submit it to you. Help me to have your perspective when my anger flares up, to remind myself that you know what is really going on, and that I cannot read the minds of others. Help me to speak the truth when I am angry, sharing what I think and feel and acknowledging that what I think and feel may only be a small part of the situation. Thank you. Amen

Day 28

The strangest dream

So the chief cupbearer told Joseph his dream. He said to him, "In my dream I saw a vine in front of me, and on the vine were three branches. As soon as it budded, it blossomed, and its clusters ripened into grapes. Pharaoh's cup was in my hand, and I took the grapes, squeezed them into Pharaoh's cup and put the cup in his hand."

"This is what it means," Joseph said to him. "The three branches are three days. Within three days Pharaoh will lift up your head and restore you to your position, and you will put Pharaoh's cup in his hand, just as you used to do when you were his cupbearer.

...

When the chief baker saw that Joseph had given a favorable interpretation, he said to Joseph, "I too had a dream: On my head were three baskets of bread. In the top basket were all kinds of baked goods for Pharaoh, but the birds were eating them out of the basket on my head."

"This is what it means," Joseph said. "The three baskets are three days. Within three days Pharaoh will lift off your head and impale your body on a pole. And the birds will eat away your flesh."

Genesis 40:9-19

In the year after I found out my daughter identified as trans, I wrote her several letters. I didn't know at the time of writing this book if she had ever read any of them. Only very recently did we find out for sure that she had not until this summer.

At one point during that first year I had a dream. A dream that transformed my thinking, my perspective, and helped me achieve some measure of reconciliation with some members of my family. While this dream helped me and continues to help me, it was quite challenging. I was ready for this challenge, desperate to understand what was going on and find a way to break out of despair. Had I received a dream like that the baker received with the interpretation Joseph gave, well, I am reminded of Hezekiah who on receiving the prophecy of his death, turned to God and prayed. May all of us always turn to God both in our distress and when we have cause to rejoice. I'd like to share this dream and my interpretation with you as I attempted to share it with my daughter in the following letter:

To a fellow dreamer,

This is going to be an odd letter, one where I'll be talking about rats, fish and elephants. First though I need to tell you about a dream I had recently. I don't often have dreams that stay with me, that I can't stop thinking about. Sometimes I do and I had one that I would like to share with you. Interestingly, you were in the dream though you did not play a big part.

In my dream I was in Jordan Peterson's house. You were there, and your mum, and I think I had a sense there were other people there, but that was less clear to me than your presence. Perhaps I could say that perspective was cloudy, or was lost in the fog... There was a young woman preparing a meal. Initially I thought she was Jordan's wife, but she was too young. She cut up vegetables and set the table. I sat down at the table and then realised I'd never

Day 28: The strangest dream

introduced myself to Jordan or his wife. They were still sitting on a couch, facing away from me. I got up and walked over to introduce myself. As I did, Tammy – Jordan's wife, stood and walked me away from Jordan to the other side of the room. We had an awkward introduction, attempting that European double kiss on both cheeks (well, off to the side) which I'm just not at all comfortable with. She then drew my attention to pictures in the room and said: "Isn't it strange that Jordan has all these pictures of fish?" I looked at the pictures and replied, "Those are elephants." I sat back down at the table and then Jordan and his wife sat down next to me. (You and your mum were already seated.) I still hadn't introduced myself to Jordan so reached out my hand and he took it and we introduced. But I began to be aware that he wasn't really looking at me. It was like he was uncomfortable looking straight at me, like he was embarrassed by me or something. Then I realised I wasn't looking straight at him either. That didn't seem right and so I forced myself to look straight at him and was shocked to see he looked haggard, ill.

I gradually woke up with this dream vivid in my thoughts. I quickly associated the pictures of elephants as representing elephants in the room – are you aware of that expression? Describing something that dominates everything but no-one will talk about.

I ended up discussing the dream with several people and as I did, other things began to become associated with the dream, an interpretation that seems to be useful and which I am now sharing with you and with others as I hope it will be helpful.

Prior to having that dream I had been fasting. Just for a day and then only a couple of meals. But still, I had chosen to humble myself and was asking God to speak to me. I believe the dream was a gift from God.

I had also, that previous weekend, been listening to one of Jordan Peterson's lectures. One where he discussed the book he was writing, and has now published – *Beyond Order*. In that lecture he shared on two chapters which either directly relate to the dream or which seem connected.

He described finding out that rats like to play games. Rough and tumble games – like children sometimes wrestle with their parents or peers. Interestingly, a researcher had found out that rats are very like people in that they enjoy playing games so long as they get a chance to win and feel like they are part of the community. A rat that never wins will not play the game. Why would they! A rat that never allows any other rat to win will find that they become excluded from the community. That is an awful thing to be excluded from your community.

A family member wrote and email to me this year to tell me that people don't like having conversations with me. Perhaps I should also say that Jordan uses the rat story to illustrate and introduce how games are a metaphor for social interactions and social institutions. So, anything that we humans do together can be construed as a type of game. Whether working together, building together, having a conversation or even an argument together. And that was the type of game being described – conversations. I was told that people find me combative and insinuated that I never let them win, or at least, I made it so difficult for them that they never even wanted to take part. I have to say, I found that quite hurtful. But was there some truth in it? Some, yes, and perhaps that is precisely why I found it so hurtful. But also, it was not totally true and did not account for the many conversations and discussions over decades where I have been playful in a good way and even played the game well such that I ensured everyone felt included and valued.

The truth is, Jordan Peterson wasn't in my dream. Neither was his wife. And you were not there and your mum wasn't really there either. It was all in my head. My subconscious telling me a story I needed to hear. Though again, I do feel that God either gave me this dream or allowed me to have this dream... Anyways, when I found Jordan and myself unable to look at each other, I wasn't looking at him, I was holding up a mirror to myself. It was me who looked so haggard in my dream. That was quite a shock to realise that. Deep down, I perceive myself as broken, spent, and I didn't want to face up to that. I've been aware since late last year that I'm barely coping. Yet, while that is maybe one piece of the interpretation, I think another piece relates to the email about conversations. Something is wrong and I need to face up to that and look closely and carefully. I need to listen, and pay attention. I need to reflect and consider and examine my life. And indeed, in this letter, that is part of my attempt to do so.

In his lecture, Jordan also spoke about the danger of hiding important things in the fog. When I was at school, an English teacher used to tell a story about a pirate who dismantled a bell that had been placed on rocks to warn sailors to steer clear of the danger. The boats were no longer warned about the rocks and so ran into them and the pirate would collect the goods that were washed up. But then one night a deep fog settled over the water and the pirate himself got lost and ended up dying on those very rocks he had lured so many boats onto.

In my dream it seemed to me that there were other people there in that room, but who they were and what they were saying was hidden from me. For over a year now it has been like that with many members of our wider family. Even and especially with you. I tried so many times to talk with you and you refused. I wanted desperately to know what was wrong but you kept me in the fog. It has been revealed to me since that members of our family had secret conversations behind my back. I was kept in the dark.

Jordan also shares an important insight. In our social games, we need feedback to know whether or not we are playing well. Refusing to play with someone is indeed important feedback and I was very aware that you refused to engage with me. But I did not know why. You withheld that from me. And so all I could do was guess. As it turns out, I guessed wrong. Is that my fault? No. Had you shared the truth with me, perhaps we could have found a way to move forwards together. It might not have been easy. But I wanted to find a way forwards. I still do.

There are elephants in the room of my life. Elephants in our relationships in our family. Things that loom large and dominate and no-one wants to talk about. But if we do not bring our attention to these humongous elephants, and keep them partially hidden in the fog, then they will remain slightly terrifying and perhaps be ultimately fatal to our relationships.

However, I do believe that if we can find a way to talk about these elephants in the room, then we may find they no longer dominate, but perhaps we will see them shrink until they can safely fit inside a picture, one that we can look at together and discuss and perhaps you will see a fish, and I will see an elephant, but we can share that and consider what is meant by that perspective.

Will you write to me? Share your perspective? Over the last year I have written many letters to you, though have only shared a couple. I would like a chance to share them all, but I know that in order to play this game properly, you need your chance to share. If you will share then I will try to play the game well, and perhaps we can agree on a set of rules that both of us will be able to follow and will help us in the playing of the game. Perhaps we can create a new game that will allow us both to play and feel that our contribution is valued.

    I still love you and I always will,
    Your father, here on earth at least,
    Dad

Father in heaven, you are the God who sends dreams and gives interpretations to them. You are the God who knows our past and our present and our future. Nothing is hidden from you, nothing we do or think or say. Praise you that you reveal the truth and will reveal all things. This scares me at times as I do not want everyone to know the full truth about my life, yet you already know the full truth and you forgave me. I praise you for your son Jesus who paid the price for my sin on the cross. I praise you that you want none of us to remain in sin or despair but instead call us into your freedom, your light, where darkness and lies and fog are all exposed. Help each of us to hear what you are saying to us. Help us to heed your warnings and listen to your counsel. Show us where we are weak and helpless in ourselves. May we seek you and be restored by you. Where we have failed to play well with others in this great game you have placed us, lead us to repent and recognise the needs of others and seek to bless them. Amen

Day 29 — A sacrifice of praise

Through Jesus, therefore, let us continually offer to God a sacrifice of praise—the fruit of lips that openly profess his name. And do not forget to do good and to share with others, for with such sacrifices God is pleased.
Hebrews 13:15-16

I've been reading through Leviticus, as you do, and am now into the book of Numbers. There is a lot in both books about the sacrifices the Israelites were to make to God. Burnt offerings and sin offerings and guilt offerings and fellowship offerings. Sacrifices of the first born males of the flock, sacrifices in place of the first born males of each Israelite family. Sacrifices of grain and bread and cakes. The first fruits of the harvest. Reading it, as I did all the way through, I was overwhelmed. Mostly by the sense that God was looking for a holy people, a people who would set themselves apart for him and that made me question my own place in relationship with God. Am I set apart for God? Am I holy and dedicated to him? It was too much for me and I became quite low, especially when I also started studying righteousness as the same time and my perceived lack of righteousness weighed me down.

I have found it easy to become weighed down since finding out our child identifies as trans. Depression seems always close and perhaps if I wanted I could get a clinical diagnosis of depression. However, I've resisted that because I personally don't want to take medication to numb the pain. I feel that pain is important for me at the moment. If we don't feel pain, we won't pull our hand out of the fire. If I don't feel pain, I won't keep fighting against what I believe is an evil ideology. If I don't feel pain, I might give in and give up and then who will fight for my child? Yet if I allow myself to become overwhelmed by the pain, I am unable to fight at all. This will not be for everyone and if you are feeling depressed do seek help. I spent nine months seeing a counsellor and found this very helpful to be able to talk about what I was experiencing and feeling. My wife has found anti-depressants helpful along with counselling.

Our pastor shared the above passage from the book of Hebrews this week in our church. Praise. Praise to God. Praise of God. I noted down as I listened that a sacrifice of praise can kill pride (I'm writing this while much of the Western world is celebrating the pagan festival of Pride). Praise can kill fear. Praise can motivate us out of laziness. And perhaps most of all for me right now – praise can lift us out of depression.

It is a sacrifice to praise God when we are depressed. It is a sacrifice to praise God when we are afraid. It is a sacrifice to praise God when we are tempted to a prideful attitude. Praise is an act of humbling ourselves, an act of worship to God that acknowledges him as our lord, our ruler, our king.

To speak words of praise in spite of the terror we might feel for our children, to sing songs of worship to God while our world appears to be coming to an end, this can reorient us out of a dark place, can give us hope, can sustain us. I often find myself thinking that God doesn't need our praise – but we do need to praise him. We benefit far more from choosing to praise God than he does, so would it not be better for me if I did it more?

We can speak words of praise to God, we can sing

Day 29: A sacrifice of praise

songs of praise, and we can also follow some of the practices the Israelites were commanded to do. I've found it strange reading that the Israelites were commanded to give a wave offering to the Lord – to hold up their sacrifices and wave them before God:

Count off fifty days up to the day after the seventh Sabbath, and then present an offering of new grain to the Lord. From wherever you live, bring two loaves made of two-tenths of an ephah of the finest flour, baked with yeast, as a wave offering of firstfruits to the Lord.
Leviticus 23:16-17

Isn't that a picture though of what a grateful child does: holds up their painting or the craft project or even the gift we have just bought them and they wave it in front of us – their parent – look at me Daddy, look at me Mummy, look at this thing I made, this gift you bought me. And our hearts melt at the delight, to see them share this wonderful thing with us. Does God also feel delight when we wave what we are thankful for at him? I am sure he does. Would it be good for us now and then to hold up something and wave it at God and say thank you, I'm delighted with this, share in my delight.

Father in heaven, I praise you. I thank you and praise you for my child. I thank you that you gave my child to me as a gift, you blessed me with my child. I praise you that despite my child's attacks, the lies, the conspiracy of many towards my family, that you are still God and you still care both for me and for my child, even for those who have become enemies towards my family. Your love is broad and deep and wide. You have loved me in spite of all the reasons I gave you to stop. You caused the sun to shine on me and the rain to fall, you caused me to prosper when I gave you no reason to bless me. You are a generous God. Amen

Day 30

Letting go

Then Jesus went with his disciples to a place called Gethsemane, and he said to them, "Sit here while I go over there and pray." He took Peter and the two sons of Zebedee along with him, and he began to be sorrowful and troubled. Then he said to them, "My soul is overwhelmed with sorrow to the point of death. Stay here and keep watch with me."
Going a little farther, he fell with his face to the ground and prayed, "My Father, if it is possible, may this cup be taken from me.
Yet not as I will, but as you will."
Matthew 26:36-39

My father shared with me a chapter – The Prayer of Relinquishment – from a book by Catherine Marshall – *Adventures in Prayer*. Family and friends share things with us to help us and oftentimes I can't accept that help, or perhaps won't accept that help. I think that over the last few years several people have tried to tell me that I needed to give up the situation with my child to God. My father may well have said this to me on more than one occasion. And I have listened. And I think I have even tried to do it. But it is one thing to say I give this up to God, it is another to do it.

Last night, before I actually read the chapter, I had been mulling over my father's words. He had shared what he was sending and that he thought it would be helpful for me to read. A prayer of relinquishment. Letting go. My wife and I have been trying in recent months to pray each evening for our children. It is difficult to know what to pray for when you are estranged. You get little news if at all. There is a world of possibilities and often the fears take hold of me. Fear. How could I let go of my children? Wouldn't I have to let go of my fear for them? What if it is my fear that drives me to pray for them? Isn't that a good thing? Perhaps not. Does fear lead to hope? Hope is a word I've heard a lot this week. In a TV show we've been watching. I see patterns everywhere and just because I hear a word in many contexts does not mean God is speaking to me. Though maybe sometimes he is.

> ***Not only so, but we also glory in our sufferings, because we know that suffering produces perseverance; perseverance, character; and character, hope. And hope does not put us to shame, because God's love has been poured out into our hearts through the Holy Spirit, who has been given to us.***
> ***Romans 5:3-5***

My attempts to study righteousness led me to the book of Romans and of course in Romans Paul writes that suffering produces perseverance, which produces character, and character produces hope. I want to hope for my children, not live in fear for them. And I have been afraid. Terribly afraid. They have not just turned from us, but also seem to have turned from God, and there is a terrible consequence if someone turns from God. Early on after my child finally revealed she identified as trans I had to face the possibility I might be unable to stop her harming herself. I was aware then that she may indeed do all the terrible things I could imagine. And in the end, if she did, I would still want her to return to us and to God. I may at that point have tried to relinquish her to God. But if I did, how many times after did I claim her back?

Last night, I found myself struggling again with this decision – do I let go of my child, of all my children and give them up to God? Did I attempt to control them from afar, demanding of God what he do? I know, I have known for so long – they each have their own free will. God will not violate that. Just as he will not violate my free will or yours. And that is why our world is in such a mess, because we all have free will and can follow whatever is in our hearts. Hearts that have the knowledge of both good and evil desires, and how often does evil win out?

Again last night, I gave my children up to God. I somehow need to accept that, live with that, and so this morning I found myself at a loss and praying for God's help. I may need to continue to pray the same prayer until finally it sticks.

Father in heaven, I let go of my children to you. I give them up to you. Help me to let go, to relinquish them to you. They belong to you. They always have, but I acknowledge I have tried to cling on to them, to control them. They are your responsibility. Please, whatever your will is for them, I choose to trust in you. I will continue to bless your name. I will love you. And I will love them. I long to be reconciled with them and I ask that you will work to make this happen. I put my trust in you. I believe you only want good for my children. I also believe that they can reject you in spite of that and choose what is evil. Jesus warned that our family may not listen, yet I choose to believe that your Holy Spirit can convict and cling onto the teaching that it is your kindness that leads us to repentance. Show your kindness to my children and lead them back to you. Amen

Day 31 — They cried out to the Lord

The Israelites did evil in the eyes of the Lord; they forgot the Lord their God and served the Baals and the Asherahs. The anger of the Lord burned against Israel so that he sold them into the hands of Cushan-Rishathaim king of Aram Naharaim, to whom the Israelites were subject for eight years. But when they cried out to the Lord, he raised up for them a deliverer, Othniel son of Kenaz, Caleb's younger brother, who saved them.
Judges 3:7-9

I am quite sure that any parent reading this book who has a child struggling with a trans identity will have cried out to the Lord. Why! Why me, why us! Please rescue us! Save our child! This passage in the book of Judges may be a difficult read. If we start reading the book of Judges we find that Israel had been led to conquer the promised land of Canaan. Some of the tribes living there had been destroyed, others had been driven out. These are challenging accounts for our modern minds. If you live, as I do, in the UK, we have known peace my whole lifetime. Yes, our soldiers have gone off to war in other countries, yet for us in our land, you have to go back to 1945, almost eighty years ago to the last time our country was at risk in a time of war. There are still some alive today who remember that last war. Who recall the bombs falling down on London and other cities, who even fought on the front line in Europe. Eventually though, they will pass away and we will have a generation that not only has not known war, but also has no direct connection to those who fought and those who suffered. We are told it was like this for Israel. Those who had fought to conquer Canaan died away and the generation that came after did not know war. Worse though, they forgot who God was, the God who had saved their ancestors from slavery, who had fought for them, giving them the land they lived in. And surrounded by pagan nations, the Israelites turned away from God and turned to the idols and the pagan practices of those nations that had not been driven out.

I see around me this pattern being repeated in the UK and other Western countries. Former Christian nations, we have embraced multi-culturalism and with it, the worship of foreign gods. Alongside that, the rejection of God's commands, the unmooring of truth, and a gradual descent into madness. The Israelites did evil. I understand that Baal worship involved child sacrifice. Is it too much of a stretch to contrast what we are doing to our children through gender affirmation and celebration of trans identity with the sacrifice of children practised by the Canaanite nations?

I have been struck by how many parents, who do not appear to have any religious belief, describe trans as evil. There is a recognition many of us have, whether Christian or Atheist, whether believer in a god or agnostic, that what our children have been led into is evil. A lie, from start to finish, that leads to harm. Drugs and hormones that will permanently impact our child's young body. Risks of sterilisation, stunted brain development, brittle bones – just some of the effects of these drugs and hormones. Then there are the surgeries. Surgeries that in many cases will lead to permanent pain. Infections. Rotting wounds. Loss of sexual function, loss of ability to conceive children of their own, loss of ability to nurse a newborn baby. These are major losses and what is promised in exchange?

A lie that all this will resolve the crippling anxiety and distress the young person felt. How different is this from the lie that offering a sacrifice to an idol would resolve anything?

In the account I quote from above, the Israelites suffered under foreign rule for eight years. This seems quite similar to the accounts of other parents whose stories I have listened to or read. So many children remain subject to this trans identity for such a long time. My own child may also have been struggling with a trans identity for many years. We are approaching the three-year anniversary of when we were told, but how long before that had she been believing this lie? We don't yet know. Are we past the half way point of this nightmare, or will we have even longer to go than the eight years Israel suffered?

We have cried out to the Lord. Why hasn't he answered us? Some might claim this is proof that our God is no different to an idol of wood or stone. We cry out. We are met with silence. I don't know why. Yet I do know that this is just how it is at times. So many similar accounts scattered in the book of Judges and in the other accounts of the history of Israel. They were in Egypt for 400 years and it is not clear to me how many of those years Israel was enslaved. Was God not listening then? I believe he was. I believe he hears every cry from our lips and the silent screams in our thoughts, the weeping of our hearts. Perhaps we are being tested. Perhaps we are being refined. Or maybe our loving God is simply waiting for our child to mature to the point where they will be willing to listen to his Holy Spirit. If God will not force you or me to obey him, why would he force our child?

Then there is the harsh truth that all of us are punished for the sins of others, by the sins of others. We live in a world full of sin and evil and that sin and evil has both direct and indirect consequences. As our culture has rejected God's truth, that we are made in the image of God and that image is male and female, so our culture has embraced a lie — that there are a multiplicity of gender identities, that we have an innate gender identity that may or may not correspond with our physical body. And the most wicked lie of all — that in order to become our true identity, some of us have to carve up our body.

What is it going to take for us to see God save us and our children? All we are told in the passage above is that Israel cried out to the Lord. We don't just have the passage above though. We have all the teaching of Jesus, of his apostles. We have the prophecies and the accounts of the kings of Israel. We have the books of the law including the account of creation. Together we find in this marvellous collection of writing both wisdom and hope. It may take years of crying out to the Lord to receive an answer, yet this long time, if it is a long time, does not have to be without value. I believe God is working in me. Yes, refining me, though that seems to be a long and arduous process. It may be that God allows our suffering in order that we will have compassion for others who are suffering. I'm uncomfortable with that statement though. Perhaps it would be better to remind ourselves of Paul's great statement:

And we know that in all things God works for the good of those who love him, who have been called according to his purpose.
Romans 8:28

In all things God works for the good of those who love him, who are called by him. Even in this time of evil. Even if our child goes ahead with life changing surgeries or treatments. God is still working for our good. And if we will look to him, if we will cry out to him, eventually he will answer. The answer may not be as we expect. Yet it will be for our good.

Our Father in heaven does not promise we will not suffer, does not assure us our children will not suffer. Jesus' warnings on this were very clear.

And he said, "The Son of Man must suffer many things and be rejected by the elders, the chief priests and the teachers of the law, and he must be killed and on the third day be raised to life."
Then he said to them all: "Whoever wants to be my disciple must deny themselves and take up their cross daily and follow me. For whoever wants to save their life will lose it, but whoever loses their life for me will save it.
Luke 9:22-24

Just as Jesus knew he would suffer and die, he warned those who followed him that they too would face suffering and some would face death. He warned others that following him would lead to a life without material comforts:

Jesus replied, "Foxes have dens and birds have nests, but the Son of Man has no place to lay his head."
Luke 9:58

To everyone he warned that we all face a choice – to take the easy road or the hard road:

"Enter through the narrow gate. For wide is the gate and broad is the road that leads to destruction, and

> *many enter through it. But small is the gate and narrow the road that leads to life, and only a few find it.*
> *Matthew 7:13-14*

We are not promised an end to suffering in this life, only that God will not abandon us. And that even though we walk a road that seems to be through the very valley of death, Jesus walks by our side, sharing our burden:

> *"Come to me, all you who are weary and burdened, and I will give you rest. Take my yoke upon you and learn from me, for I am gentle and humble in heart, and you will find rest for your souls. For my yoke is easy and my burden is light."*
> *Matthew 11:28-30*

I would love to be able to give you a method to ensure your prayers will be answered, a three-step plan that you could follow. Instead I can only tell you the truth. God loves you. God loves your child. God will not force our children. God hears the cry of our hearts and the cries that we utter. Crying out to the Lord is not a waste of our time or God's. God will use this time of suffering, if we will let him.

Father in heaven, hear the cry of our hearts, hear our prayers for our children. If you will not force us and will not force them, how should we pray? Please teach us, Father, teach us how to pray for our children so that you will be delighted and quick to answer. Help us to humble ourselves and deal with any sin that may cause you to turn away from us. Give us your wisdom and discernment to understand the advice given by

Jesus and your many servants throughout the long years. Rescue our family. Save us from this evil. Show us what to do. Comfort us and comfort our children that if they are anxious and afraid and this is driving them to harm their body, that they will not longer feel that compulsion. Set our children free from the lies of the evil one. Help them to perceive truth and discern good from evil. Do not give up on us, and give us strength that we will stand firm in you. Amen

Your Invitation

*"For God so loved the world
that he gave his one and only Son,
that whoever believes in him
shall not perish but have eternal life."*
John 3 v 16

Almost forty years ago I was challenged to respond to the call of Jesus. I believe this world is not all there is. That this world was created by God, and that we, his creation turned away from him. The experience of having my children turn away from me has maybe given me a small insight into how God feels that so many of us ignore him, fail to appreciate him, fail to acknowledge all he has done for us and given us. And yet God still loves us! But he will not let us, his children, take him for a fool. It is not an easy thing to accept that we will not all be welcomed by God, that many of us will face him on the final day of judgement only to find he turns away and says, "I never knew you." Jesus' statement above, that God loves the world, is tempered by the warning that those who believe in him will not perish. This implies that those who do not believe in Jesus will perish. Paul wrote:

For all have sinned and fall short of the glory of God
Romans 3 v 23

Sin. Not a nice word. It means to fall short, to miss the target. All of us fail to live up to what God calls us to. This separates us from God. We can admit this and accept Jesus' offer to make up the difference. Or we can say, I don't need you, Jesus. And Jesus warns that those who choose this will be given what they want and be thrown out from God's presence, into Hell. Jesus will not force any of us to love him or follow him. He invites us to take up our cross and accept him as Lord over our lives. If you have never accepted his invitation, and would like to do so, then would you do so by praying this prayer now:

Father in heaven, I know that I am a sinner. I want to turn from my sins, and I ask for your forgiveness. I believe that Jesus Christ is your Son. I believe He died for my sins and that You raised Him to life. I want Jesus to come into my heart and to take control of my life. Fill me with your Holy Spirit. I choose to trust Jesus as my Saviour and follow Him as my Lord from this day forward. Amen

A Final Word

Thank you for reading. If you are going through any of what I have experienced, my heart goes out to you. There are some suggested resources after this section, books and websites and groups I have found helpful. There are a growing number of helpful resources now, some of which did not exist three years ago. I encourage you to seek help, and also advise you to be discerning. Not everyone has you or your child's best interests in mind.

My wife and I could not have survived the last three years without the support of my parents and my sister, and the support of close friends in our church. To them and all those who listened and tried to understand what we were going through, who did not jump to affirm our daughter but instead heard our concerns, thank you!

Thank you to Bayswater Support Group! A safe space to share and vent and know that others understand.

Thank you to Psalm 121 Dads, you know who you are! Thank you for listening, for sharing your stories and your many prayers and words of encouragement.

Thank you to my counsellor, who listened and helped me process such a confusing time.

Thank you to my managers and colleagues who listened without judging me.

Thank you again to Nathaniel Dasco for another excellent book cover template used on this book.

If anyone feels able to leave a review of this book online, anonymously or publicly, that would be very much appreciated.

Find me online at:
https://goal31.substack.com
https://www.goal31.co.uk

Resources

The Cass Review – Independent Review of gender identity services for children and young people:
https://cass.independent-review.uk/home/publications/final-report/

The WPATH Files by Mia Hughes and Michael Shellenberger:
https://public.substack.com/p/the-wpath-files

Detransitioner Interviews:
Sinead Watson: https://youtu.be/p90K88EdOXs
Ritchie Herron: https://youtu.be/tk7NX7iPr9k
Prisha Mosley: https://youtu.be/dY6s_wIDUaU

Recommended books:
Irreversible Damage by Abigail Shrier
Time To Think by Hannah Barnes
Trans by Helen Joyce
When Kids Say They Are Trans by Sasha Ayad, Lisa Marchiano, and Stella O'Malley
Desist, Detrans & Detox by Maria Keffler
Parents with Inconvenient Truths about Trans edited by Josie A. and Dina S.

Organisations and websites:
https://www.bayswatersupport.org.uk/
https://genspect.org/
https://www.transgendertrend.com/
https://www.pittparents.com/

Other books by this author

Non-Fiction

31 Days of Prayer

Prayer helps. It calms the spirit and relieves our anxiety. It allows us to commune with the God who created us, with our Father in heaven. At times of great crisis, it is common for people to turn to God in prayer. But what should we pray?

Repent is a word out of fashion. It conjures up images of preachers shouting of hell-fire and brimstone. Yet when you read the bible, a very different message can be seen. Underneath and behind every call to repentance is God's love, God's desire that we be reunited with him, his determination that we not be lost, but find life, and experience this life and the next to the full. That we experience the kingdom of heaven, here on earth, and prepare for the next life with our father God.

31 days to study what God's word says about repentance, about the kingdom of heaven, and then to turn daily to God in prayer. Will you accept the challenge?

The Commands of Jesus
31 Days of Prayer – Book Two

Christians call Jesus Lord, and sing praises to him declaring he is King, yet how much time have we taken to understand what our King has commanded us to do? We say God is love, God is merciful, God is kind and indeed he is all these things, yet when reading the bible, we find many examples of God commanding his people, and Jesus continuing to do the same to his disciples.

Following on from 31 Days of Prayer, this 31 day study and devotional guide will help you to understand that the commands Jesus gives us to follow are not simply burdens and drudgery to obey, but a pathway to a more content life, one where we are brought closer to our heavenly father's presence and will allow us to be better able to live our lives in peace and in good will with those around us.

Each day's devotional begins with one of the passages from Jesus' teaching. Stories from the author's life are shared along with questions and quotes from relevant passages throughout the bible. Each command is discussed and examined to give insight into the relevance of Jesus' commands to our lives today. The commands of Jesus are a challenge and a blessing and will give you a deeper understanding of Jesus' call on your life.

Double Your Salary
...without losing your soul!

A Motivational Memoir

An account of one man's attempt to transform his life, placing God first, and seeking to grow and learn in order to provide for his family.

Double Your Salary ...without losing your soul! offers a balanced perspective on the relationship between the urgency of providing for our needs, with the necessity of making time for family, friends, and faith.

Filled with prompts and suggestions to get you thinking about your own future, encouraging you to set goals and to develop a plan that could transform your life.

There is a common belief that only governments can reduce poverty. Double Your Salary offers you an alternative: you can take control of your career, your future, your life!

Fiction

Fallen Warriors
A Christian Thriller

In the city of York, a young nurse dies in a tragic accident but is mysteriously brought back to life. As she attempts to find out and understand what happened, a group of ordinary people find themselves drawn together: a homeless man tormented by his past, a thief who has crossed a dangerous line, a young Muslim girl searching for answers, a detective hiding a secret, a woman who wants to remove the pastor of her church. Unknown to any of them, an Islamic group secretly plots to form a new Caliphate in the centre of England. York becomes the battle ground for the largest terrorist attack ever faced in the West. Fallen warriors are called to stand and fight, but will they stand or will they fall?

The Great Scottish Land Grab
A Scottish Novel

When his wife is threatened while on a walking holiday in the Scottish Highlands, Robert Castle tries to get justice, only to find the people of Scotland have little rights on their historic land.

Meanwhile, Scotland is preparing to vote on independence when the deaths of senior members of the Scottish Government forces an election.

Disillusioned by his research into Scotland's history, and sensing that the theft of Scotland's land over many centuries has robbed the people of their opportunity to be independent, Castle establishes a new political party and fights for a modern-day land grab – to reverse the clearances and return the land that was stolen from Scotland's people.

Challenging an out of touch parliament, Robert turns government on its head by introducing Cafe Politics – a way for communities to debate and agree their own policies.

But how far will Robert go in his determination to overturn the injustice of the Highland Clearances, and will he lead Scotland to a better future or into civil war?

About the Author

A husband, and father to three adult children, Mark Anderson Smith is a Christian writer. Since finding out his youngest daughter identified as trans, he has campaigned to raise awareness of the dangers children and young people face from gender affirmation. As many parents in a similar situation choose to do, such campaigning has been done anonymously out of a desire to prevent a widening rift between himself and his child and other members of his family. Over the last three years he has given testimony to the Scottish Parliament, been quoted anonymously in several leading UK newspapers, and shared his story to colleagues in his workplace. After three years, his daughter having cut off all contact despite repeated efforts on his behalf to reconcile, being aware that she is harming herself and plans to undergo a dangerous, non-reversible surgery, Mark has decided to publicly share his perspective as a father in this book, in the hope that other parents might find some encouragement in their own struggles.

Mark currently works as a Business Analyst, helping clients define requirements for business system improvements and changes, and working with software developers to implement those changes. He has enjoyed a successful career as an independent software developer prior to his current role, developing complex systems for clients such as Prudential, Sky, BBC, Hilton Hotels and others.

His Christian faith has been a strong influence throughout his life. In 2009 he accepted a challenge to write down 100 goals. His thirty first goal was the inspiration for his company: Goal 31 Ltd, and in many ways for this book: "To be and do all that God wants of me."

Made in the USA
Coppell, TX
31 January 2025